EXPERTISE, EXPERIENCE & EMPATHY

EXPERTISE, EXPERIENCE & EMPATHY

Rewiring Strategy,
Talent and Leadership
for the Age of AI

JAMIE PRIDE

Voices from the frontlines

'Artificial intelligence has created considerable anxiety among boards and senior business leaders, driven by misunderstanding and an inability to move beyond established business practices. In this book, Jamie Pride addresses these concerns with clarity and pragmatism, demonstrating how AI can reshape and reconfigure business models for the future. AI is real, present and a critical part of our future.'

Mike Smith – Former CEO, ANZ Banking Group

'As AI reshapes how work is done, this book reframes the issue leaders actually need to solve. The challenge is discipline: what to automate, what must remain human, and how to preserve experience, judgement and trust as organisations grow. A serious guide for leaders who need decisions and organisations to hold up under real consequence.'

Craig Scroggie – CEO and Managing Director,
NEXTDC Limited (ASX: NXT)

'Jamie Pride is, and has always been, a thought leader and one of the best over-the-horizon thinkers. He has been one of the first people in the Australian business community to focus on the application of AI and understand the benefits and challenges that AI poses for companies.

'In *Expertise, Experience & Empathy*, he addresses the implications for organisational design and looks at the reshaping of talent in a world dominated by AI. This book takes AI out of the hypothetical and provides boards and executives with a practical guide as they reshape their businesses. In addition, it makes the reader reflect on their own readiness for the future.'

John Meacock – Former Global Strategy Officer, Deloitte

'*Expertise, Experience & Empathy* captures something I've felt but rarely seen articulated so clearly. While AI collapses the value of "knowing" – where accessing expertise is instant – it also erodes the experiences that build judgement. This book powerfully reframes why judgement, learning through consequence and trust become the true sources of enduring advantage in an AI-first world. It is essential reading for leaders shaping their organisations for this new era.'

Jeremy Cooper – Vice President, Asia Pacific and Japan, Databricks

'Having built a business of scale during the first major wave of disruption (the start of the internet), I've seen how technology totally resets the rules of the game. Jamie Pride brilliantly captures why this new tidal wave of disruption is different: when AI makes expertise a commodity, human judgement and trust become the only true differentiators. This book is an essential, high-stakes playbook for any leader who wants to successfully navigate AI disruption without losing their organisation's soul.'

Adrian Critchlow – Co-founder, Booking.com

'This book is an essential guide for the new way to lead in an AI-powered world. It will shift your focus from just doing work faster to surfacing the unique value of being human – making better decisions and building the kind of deep-seated trust that will be the only true competitive advantage in the years to come.'

Brigid Archibald – Vice President, Japan and Asia Pacific, Miro

'This book is a "war memoir" directly from the front lines of the AI revolution. It gets to the heart of the challenge executives fear most: how do I preserve what makes my organisation distinctive in the face of AI? Jamie provides practical insights and an optimistic pathway for making deliberate choices about the critical roles that humans must still play, and how organisations should configure to remain relevant to customers. It is a must-read for any executive.'

Ian McCall – Former Lead Strategy Partner, Deloitte Asia Pacific

'Jamie has landed one cracker of a book, pulling leadership out of glossy keynotes and dropping it into the messy human reality of work. He's captured the issues of AI with ruthless simplicity. The value of expertise drops to zero, experience isn't mystical, it's accumulated, and there has never been a time when empathy will be the most important accelerant of trust. Blending hard-won know-how with disarming honesty and self-effacing wit makes this a rollicking read. If there is one lesson to remember, it's that AI is the new competitive chemistry – it's a powerful wildfire ripping through borders at a speed we have never seen before. Ultimately, the winners will be those who lead with clarity, humanity and are brutally honest that they are already on a burning platform.'

Karen Lawson – CEO, VC, NED and Investor | Former Managing Director, Spotify ANZ, and Peloton Interactive

'This isn't another book about AI – it's a book about real leadership and critical thinking in the evolving world of AI. It dispenses with the hype and provides frameworks for leaders to develop, evaluate and test strategies for the new era. If you want to move beyond "AI fanfare and innovation theatre" and focus on building resilient and transformed businesses, this is your guide.'

Scott Thomson – Former Head of Innovation, Google

'*Expertise, Experience & Empathy* is a definitive blueprint for navigating our AI-driven reality. Jamie Pride masterfully approaches the critical importance of human skills that AI can never replace. He provides a vital roadmap for turning human perspectives into a competitive advantage for a positive future. An essential guide for anyone looking to sharpen their critical thinking and perspective to remain authentic and decisive in a rapidly evolving world.'

Bianca Scheffler – Head of Artificial Intelligence, KPMG Switzerland

For Phoebe, Harrison and Imogen.

You will live and work in an AI world.

I hope this helps you stay unmistakably human.

First published in 2026 by Jamie Pride

A catalogue entry for this book is available from the National Library of Australia.

PB ISBN: 978-1-923630-20-8
HB ISBN: 978-1-923630-24-6

Book production and text design by Publish Central

Disclaimer

The material in this publication is of the nature of general comment only and does not represent professional advice. It is not intended to provide specific guidance for particular circumstances, and it should not be relied on as the basis for any decision to take action or not take action on any matter which it covers. Readers should obtain professional advice where appropriate, before making any such decision. To the maximum extent permitted by law, the author and associated entities and publisher disclaim all responsibility and liability to any person, arising directly or indirectly from any person taking or not taking action based on the information in this publication.

Contents

The evolving currency of human work 1

Chapter 1: Work, rewired 5

Chapter 2: The human edge 27

Chapter 3: Who's in the cockpit? 53

Chapter 4: Shift happens 77

Chapter 5: Strategy before tools 103

Chapter 6: Scalpels need surgeons 125

Chapter 7: From intent to impact 145

Chapter 8: Trains, planes and disruption 167

Chapter 9: Built for intelligence 187

After expertise 209

Getting in touch 215

To those who made it happen 217

INTRODUCTION

The evolving currency of human work

Early in the summer of 2020, I was sitting at my computer, drinking a glass of red, staring in disbelief at the screen. That day, a colleague at Western Sydney University had mentioned an application in the machine-learning space that she said I should check out. I had spent the next few hours using a basic command-line interface to produce paragraphs of text. I'd then cut and paste that text into a well-known plagiarism checker – only to be told time and time again that the output was original.[1] I poured another glass of wine and ran another series of tests. I still couldn't believe what I was seeing. How could an algorithm produce such original and 'intelligent' writing? As a management consultant, part-time university lecturer and semi-professional writer, I knew this was huge, and things were

1 A note on my use of dashes here feels pertinent. Dashes have been used throughout this book as a considered style choice – and I've been using them since long before they were claimed to be a telltale sign someone was using ChatGPT. Sometimes a dash is just a dash.

going to quickly change – big time. That application was GPT-2, and it was very limited – used mainly as a proof of concept by machine-learning academics and a handful of enthusiasts. By June that year, GPT-3 would be released. Then, two years later in November 2022, came the big one – ChatGPT. The rest is history.

As I sit down to write this book, AI is mainstream. Colleagues at work discuss 'frontier models' and LLMs, while names such as Claude, Gemini and OpenAI are everyday terms. Over the past two years, I have worked with some of the world's largest organisations to help them work out how this new technology will impact their markets, strategy and, most importantly, their workforce. I have seen the good, the bad and the ugly when it comes to the use of AI in large corporations. But above all else, sits a question nobody is quite ready to ask: 'If AI can do this, what am I here for?'

That question is becoming harder to ignore.

The first sign that work was changing did not arrive as a breakthrough or a headline. It arrived as a feeling. Leaders who once spoke with crisp certainty started to pause mid-sentence, sensing that something had shifted underneath them.

For most of the last century, expertise was the golden ticket. If you needed answers, you sought out the people who had them: the doctor, the lawyer, the consultant. Knowledge was rare, and that rarity made it valuable. Entire industries grew around this scarcity. Universities built empires on it. Consultants wrapped themselves in rituals to signal it. The expert was the person who held the keys to the kingdom.

Now knowledge is everywhere – searchable, summarised and served through a prompt. AI has democratised expertise.

What once required years of study can now be delivered in seconds. Early AI was referred to as an 'expert system' for a reason: it promised to codify the knowledge of experts and specialists. That promise has finally arrived. The cost of producing an acceptable answer has collapsed, and the distance between junior and senior has narrowed in strange, uneven ways.

If you are looking to buy expertise, it is happy days. The price of expertise is trending towards zero. If you are selling it, things are about to get ugly.

The same tasks that once built careers now take minutes. The activities that once defined competence now look like table stakes. The rituals of expertise have lost their power, yet the expectations on professionals have climbed. Accountants, lawyers, analysts, designers, consultants, engineers: whole careers have been built on the ability to charge for what you know. But in a world where almost everything is knowable, what keeps you and your organisation valuable? What protects your edge when AI knows as much as you do and learns far faster?

That is the challenge at the heart of this book.

AI has not eliminated the need for human contribution. It has simply reordered where that contribution sits. The real value has migrated, moving from the work of knowing to the work of deciding. **Value has shifted from the mechanics of execution to the messiness of judgement, and from technical precision to the quiet art of showing empathy and being trusted when the stakes feel personal.**

This migration is not a metaphor. It shows up in balance sheets, margin pressure and the silent anxiety of people who built their identity around capabilities that AI now performs without complaint. It shows up in the executive who realises their best team member is already leaning on AI for everything, and in the consultant who wonders why clients hesitate when the proposal arrives – thinking they can probably do this themselves using AI. The old signals of mastery no longer convince.

What remains is harder to codify but impossible to ignore. It is the ability to interpret signals that do not fit the pattern, to weigh trade-offs when every option carries risk, to hold steady when others feel uncertain and to navigate conversations where empathy matters more than accuracy. These are not new skills. They have always mattered. But they were rarely the centre of the work. Now they are the work.

This book maps that transition. It shows where the value of human work now lives, and outlines how to build organisations, careers and strategies around it. It offers frameworks that clarify the shift, guardrails that prevent capability erosion and practical systems that turn intention into action. It is written for leaders who sense the ground moving and want to act before the structure gives way.

The path ahead demands discipline. Automation will accelerate. Models will improve. Expectations will climb. The organisations that thrive will not be the ones with the most AI. They will be the ones who understand what AI cannot touch and design everything else around protecting it. They will be the ones who recognise that intelligence has entered the system, but judgement still requires a human.

The future of work does not belong to the people who know the most. It belongs to the people who can make the best decisions and be trusted most when it matters.

That future of human work starts here.

CHAPTER 1

Work, rewired

I was staring at the ceiling, alone, in a hospital room in Invercargill, on the South Island of New Zealand. This is not where I normally do my best thinking – and especially not in this case, given the number of painkillers I was on. Three weeks earlier, I'd had an emergency gallbladder extraction back home in Sydney. Then, in a moment of questionable judgement, I decided I should still attend a writers' retreat in Queenstown.

What. An. Idiot.

One helicopter medical evacuation and two surgeries later, I'd seen the inside of a few too many hospitals and met a small parade of doctors and surgeons. They were calm, competent and annoyingly well-rested. They also had to put up with me, which is no small thing. I am not a good patient. I like reasons. I like options. And I like control. Hospitals offer gowns that don't close properly and nurses who wake you up five times a night to check your vitals. It is, objectively, a hostile environment for my personality type.

When you're stuck in a hospital room, time expands. And if you're me, you fill that time with YouTube. So, deciding I should be more productive, I did what any sensible person would do in a medical crisis. I opened my AI doctor of choice – 'Chatty G', as I affectionately call him. What else would an AI nerd do?

I started a new chat and quickly uploaded blood test results and medical images. I asked questions that were equal parts practical and slightly neurotic. What does this number mean? Is that normal? What should I be watching for? What would you do next? The responses came back instantly. They were clear, structured and calm. If I ignored the fact I was communicating with an algorithm, I felt like I had a personal surgeon on call – and a surgeon who never slept, became impatient or said, 'Let's just wait and see'. It was fantastic.

And then, after the initial novelty wore off, something became painfully obvious. Yes, the AI had an endless supply of expertise. It could explain the physiology, interpret ranges, summarise possible causes, list treatment paths, and even tell me which questions to ask the next doctor. It could do the technical component of the work with the cheerfulness of a Golden Retriever and the thoroughness of an anxious accountant.

But it had no experience. It had never sat in a hospital room at 3 am with a patient who is trying to decide whether a new symptom is 'interesting' or 'the beginning of something catastrophic'. It had never watched a surgeon make a call with imperfect information and full responsibility. It had never had to choose between two options – both of which are defensible, but one of which is wrong in a way you only discover later.

Most importantly, it suffered no consequences. It could offer possibilities all day long because it will never have to live with the outcomes. It never has to face your family. It never has to sign the discharge papers. It never has to carry the quiet moral weight that comes with saying, 'This is what I think we should do'.

That is the difference between knowledge and judgement.

In that hospital room, it hit me with surprising force: AI can make expertise abundant, but it cannot make experience cheap. And when the stakes are high, people do not just want answers. They want someone who can decide, and someone they can trust while the decision is being made.

In other words, the value isn't in what the system knows. It's in how the decision gets made, and how you feel about the person making it.

The centre of gravity of professional work is shifting. When knowledge becomes abundant, value moves from being based on what you know to how you decide and to, ultimately, why people trust you. Expertise still counts, but experience and empathy now do the heavy lifting. The people and organisations that understand this early will adapt. Those that cling to the old mechanisms of value will not.

Deconstructing work

As part of my consulting work, I spend an inordinate amount of time thinking about how work actually gets done. Not how work is described in job descriptions or organisational charts, but how it really happens on a Tuesday afternoon when something breaks.

Clients tend to ask variations of the same questions. What roles do we still need? What should we automate? Should we stop hiring altogether or, if we do hire, what skills will matter in the future? While these might sound like workforce questions, they are not. They are questions about value.

To answer them properly, you have to take work apart. You have to strip it back to its components and ignore the comforting labels we have built around roles and professions. When you do that, a simple pattern emerges.

All work, when you reduce it far enough, is made up of three things: expertise, experience and empathy. This is what I call the 'new triad of work'. And once you see it, it becomes very difficult to unsee it.

Here's what is at the heart of each of the elements in the triad:

- **Expertise:** What you know; the codified, repeatable, technical component of work.
- **Experience:** How you apply it; the judgement, context and pattern recognition born of lived practice and its consequences.
- **Empathy:** Why people trust you to do it; the relational, ethical and empathetic dimension that sustains loyalty.

The new triad of work highlights a shift in the mechanics of value creation. When AI can deliver expertise faster than any human, your focus needs to move upstream. You and your organisation become most useful not when you know something, but when you can interpret, prioritise and decide with judgement. You become most credible not when you claim expertise, but when others feel confident that your decisions will hold under pressure. **Experience becomes the accelerator. Empathy becomes the insurance.**

The implications run through every profession. Technical skill becomes the ticket to play. Judgement becomes the differentiator. Trust becomes the backbone of every professional relationship. Leaders who still optimise for expertise alone will misread the moment. They will hire for the wrong attributes, promote for the wrong signals and measure the wrong outputs. Their organisations will struggle to adapt because they will be building capability in the area AI is already consuming. The professional of the future will not compete on what they know. They will compete on how they decide and why others trust them.

Why now: The end of expertise as advantage

AI is the greatest leveller of expertise since the printing press. When Gutenberg's machine arrived, monks lost their monopoly on copying Bibles. When the internet appeared, encyclopaedias lost their monopoly on facts. Now, AI is stripping professionals of their monopoly on knowing. The shift is not subtle. It is structural. The price of producing a competent answer has crashed, and the time taken to reach that answer has shortened from hours to seconds. The hierarchy built on who knows what is collapsing faster than most realise.

The consequences show up everywhere. A junior analyst with ChatGPT can now produce a report that once belonged to a senior consultant. A graduate lawyer can now draft a contract in seconds that once took a partner hours. Designers can generate dozens of variations before a human has even opened Photoshop. Knowledge still matters, but it no longer defines advantage. Value has moved upstream. That movement is the reason this moment feels so disorienting. The work is still there, but the path to expertise has weakened. The apprenticeship ladder has fewer rungs. The steps that once built experience are being automated. The very tasks that taught people how to decide are disappearing. For many, this is a problem.

For buyers of expertise, this feels like progress. It is deflationary magic: faster, cheaper, good-enough answers at scale. For sellers, it is something else entirely. It is margin compression. It is career compression. It is the quiet erosion of how value is priced. Professionals built their identity on being the person who knew. Organisations built their models on charging for that knowledge. Both now face a landscape where AI retrieves knowledge and delivers expertise effortlessly, yet carries none of the responsibility that makes judgement difficult.

But the deeper shift sits below the surface. As AI absorbs expertise, the shelf life of professional knowledge becomes shorter. The speed of decay increases. Technical advantage becomes a moment, not a moat. What used to differentiate professionals now simply keeps them in the game. The real advantage comes from interpretation and judgement. When everyone has the same information, the question is no longer who knows the most, but who can decide best. Judgement becomes the differentiator because it rests on lived experience, context and consequence. It requires exposure to ambiguity and the willingness to own decisions when the answer is not obvious.

Empathy rises at the same time. Trust becomes more important because clients cannot easily tell which outputs were produced by a person and which were produced by a machine. Relationship quality becomes a signal of safety. People lean towards those who make them feel understood when the environment feels unstable. In this environment, confidence becomes currency.

This is why the new triad of work matters now. AI has made expertise abundant, and in the process has thinned the pipeline of experience. When routine work disappears, so do the opportunities to learn through consequence. Judgement becomes scarce just as it becomes more important. Trust rises alongside it because people can no longer tell who is merely informed and who is genuinely capable.

The end of knowledge as advantage is not the end of professional work. It is the start of a different version.

The framework: The three layers of value

The new triad of work offers a clear way to understand where value and contribution now concentrate: expertise, experience and empathy. These three layers have always existed, but AI has reordered their importance. Expertise is no longer the hero of professional work. It is the groundwork. Experience becomes the differentiator because it converts knowledge into judgement. Empathy becomes the ultimate moat because it determines trust, legitimacy and influence. Together, they explain why the centre of gravity of work is moving, and why leaders must recalibrate how they hire, reward and design roles.

Expertise: Knowledge as commodity

Expertise once meant authority. You were an expert because you knew things others didn't. You held specialised knowledge that was hard to access, hard to acquire and hard to validate.

That scarcity created value. Professions protected it through exams, credentials and apprenticeships. Entire hierarchies were built on it.

That edge is gone. AI can now pass bar exams, summarise medical journals, analyse financials, write code and produce compliant documents at scale. It can synthesise a decade of research in moments. It can replicate a pattern across thousands of examples without fatigue. What once required years of training can now be reproduced with a prompt.

Expertise has not disappeared, but its scarcity has. Knowledge is everywhere. The barrier to entry has fallen. The baseline has risen. Clients now assume technical competence by default. They no longer pay a premium for the ability to retrieve, summarise or organise information. These tasks have migrated to the machine, and every industry feels this shift. Analysts, designers, accountants, consultants and managers all now work in an environment where being correct is no longer enough. The machine is also correct, and often faster.

This does not diminish the importance of expertise. It reframes its role. Expertise becomes the starting point rather than the differentiator. It is necessary but not sufficient. Professionals still need deep knowledge, but they no longer compete on that knowledge. They compete on what they do with it. The promise of expertise has changed from insight to assurance. It signals that your foundation is solid, but not that your viewpoint is unique.

The critical shift for leaders is recognising that expertise alone no longer creates value. In an AI-saturated world, expertise must be layered with judgement and trust. Without those layers, it becomes interchangeable – and once it becomes interchangeable, it becomes cheap.

Experience: Judgement as differentiator

When it comes to value in an AI-centric world, experience sits above expertise. It is the conversion of knowledge into judgement. It is the ability to read context, weigh trade-offs and make decisions when the answer is not obvious. It emerges from repeated exposure to real consequences. Experience comes from doing, failing, adjusting and trying again. It is shaped by patterns, nuance and the subtle signals that only reveal themselves over time.

Experience is what happens when knowledge meets reality. It is why a senior leader can scan a situation and sense which risks matter, which assumptions are flawed and which problems are more important than they appear. That sense is not mystical. It is accumulated. It comes from years of decisions that carried weight, from exposure to environments that did not behave as expected, and from the steady development of intuition grounded in consequence.

AI can simulate data, but it cannot suffer consequences. It can generate options, but it cannot feel the pressure of choosing between them. It cannot carry the responsibility of a decision that affects people, customers or society. It cannot navigate ambiguity when the right answer is not the optimal one, but the acceptable one. Experience is built on stakes. AI can model possibilities, but it cannot feel the weight of choosing between them.

This is why experience becomes more valuable as expertise becomes abundant. The more the machine 'knows', the more humans must decide. The more AI accelerates the flow of information, the more leaders must interpret it. The more automation removes routine work, the more complex work rises to the surface. Experience becomes a premium because nothing else can substitute for it. Early-career pathways are collapsing, and the traditional route to experience is vanishing. When the tasks that build judgement disappear, judgement becomes more valuable.

Experience also carries confidence. Clients and stakeholders look for the person who has been there before, who has navigated similar terrain and who knows which signals matter. They want assurance that their decision-maker can handle deviation, ambiguity and surprise. That assurance cannot be automated. It is earned.

Empathy: Trust as the ultimate currency

Empathy is often the least-discussed layer of work, yet it has the greatest influence. It is the layer that determines why people believe you, follow you and pay a premium for your decisions. This layer includes trust, ethics, reliability and relational skills. It shapes the confidence others place in your judgement.

Without empathy and trust, professional relationships collapse. People buy with emotion and explain with logic. They choose advisers, leaders and partners based on how those people make them feel. They seek out the individuals who bring calm during uncertainty, who communicate with clarity and who signal integrity when the path is unclear. In a volatile environment, these emotional cues carry more weight than ever.

The Trusted Advisor model (outlined by David Maister, Charles Green and Robert Galford) captured the essence of this decades ago: trust is built not solely on brilliance, but also on reliability, intimacy and low self-orientation. The logic holds even more strongly in the age of AI. When everyone appears equally competent, people choose the person who makes them feel safest. They choose the leader who listens, who considers, who explains and who takes responsibility. They choose the team that cares enough to guide, and not just to answer.

Empathy becomes a moat because it is the hardest layer to replicate. AI can mimic warmth, but not earn trust. It can generate empathy-shaped sentences, but not sustain a relationship. It can produce predictable communication, but not the kind of connection that reassures people when the stakes feel personal. Empathy is built on credibility, humanity and consistency. It is not built on syntax.

This is why leaders cannot treat empathy and trust as a soft skill. Instead, they are structural. They govern whether people accept automation, follow decisions and adopt new ways of working. Without empathy and trust, the relationship breaks down – and expertise and experience never have the chance to matter.

How the layers work together

The three layers of the triad reinforce each other in the following ways:

- Expertise provides the base, assuring people that you know your domain.
- Experience shows that you can interpret complexity and make decisions under pressure.
- Empathy signals that your decisions will consider their needs, their risk and their context.

When the layers work together, professionals become indispensable. When one layer is missing, the system falters. For example:

- A lawyer with expertise but no emotional intelligence struggles to build loyalty.
- A consultant with experience but no trust struggles to win work.
- A leader with emotional skill but no judgement struggles to deliver outcomes.
- A professional with expertise alone competes with the machine.

The triad solves this puzzle by showing that value no longer comes from expertise alone. It is created through experience and secured through empathy.

Why leaders need the triad now

The new triad of work exposes the blind spots in traditional professional development.

Organisations still invest heavily in expertise through training, accreditation and technical development. They invest less in experience formation, which is now the scarcest resource. And they invest least in emotional capability, despite it being the most decisive in moments of uncertainty.

AI intensifies this imbalance. When expertise is automated, organisations that rely on it struggle. When experience evaporates because early-career roles are removed, workforce resilience declines. When trust is neglected, people resist change. Leaders need a model that rebalances these forces – and the triad provides that model. It clarifies where to invest, how to design roles and how to build capability that will hold under pressure.

Building capability across the triad

To apply the triad, you and your organisation must rebuild the pipeline of expertise, experience and empathy deliberately. You must treat expertise as infrastructure: vital, but not differentiating. You must cultivate experience through accelerated exposure, rotational assignments and decisions with real consequences. You must design empathy into the system by building trust, transparency and reliability into every workflow.

This is not optional. It is structural. As AI gains expertise, humans must contribute where they add unique value. That value lives in judgement and trust.

The triad as strategic lens

The new triad of work is not only a model for talent but also a strategic lens. And it provides this lens in the following ways:

- It shows leaders where to automate and where not to.
- It reveals where the organisation is vulnerable to capability erosion, and particularly the loss of judgement and experience.
- It signals where human effort adds the most value.
- It clarifies which roles and activities will rise in importance and which will fade.
- It explains why early-career design becomes critical in an era of intelligent tools.
- It anchors transformation in human advantage, not technological novelty.

When you apply the triad consistently, your organisation can navigate AI disruption without losing identity, capability or trust. You can protect the layers that matter while automating the layers that do not.

This is the heart of the framework. **Expertise is abundant. Experience is valuable. Empathy is definitive.** The organisations that understand this will thrive. The ones that cling to the old value model will be overtaken by those who see clearly where human advantage now lives.

Application: The lawyer test

Over the course of my career, I have worked with a lot of lawyers. I've worked with good ones, average ones, cheap ones and very expensive ones. Some have billed like surgeons and behaved like interns. Others have charged modestly and quietly saved the day. Across boardrooms, disputes, contracts and moments where the stakes were uncomfortably real, I've noticed a pattern. The lawyers I valued most were not always the smartest in the room. They were the ones I trusted when things went sideways. Somewhere along the way, without meaning to, I developed what I now think of as a 'lawyer test'. This isn't a formal checklist, but a simple instinctive filter for where value actually sits. And it turns out, this test maps almost perfectly to the new triad of work.

The lawyer test offers a practical way to see how the triad shows up in real decisions. It makes the abstract concrete, and can be applied across all professions. When people choose a professional, they unconsciously evaluate expertise, experience and empathy. They rarely label the process, but the pattern is consistent. The logic is simple, and the implications run far beyond law.

Expertise gets you in the door

You do not hire a lawyer who lacks the basics. You expect the person you hire to know the relevant legislation, the precedents and the structure of the argument. Drafting, searching and summarising are assumed. Competence is not impressive. It is required. You only notice it when it's missing.

AI has already raised this bar. A machine can generate a competent contract, argument or summary in seconds. It can review thousands of documents faster than any human. The baseline is now higher than most professionals realise.

Expertise still matters, but it no longer differentiates. It acts as the ticket to play, rather than the reason to pay. Clients do not reward expertise. They penalise its absence.

Experience earns confidence

Experience is where the value starts to separate, often quietly.

A good lawyer knows that the person who is right doesn't always win. Experience is the signal that your lawyer has handled cases like yours before. It is the quiet assurance that they know which risks matter, which trade-offs are acceptable and which tactics work under pressure. You pay for this lived practice.

Experience reduces risk. It tells you this person has navigated hostile judges, tense negotiations or complex disputes. It tells you they can cope when the script changes.

AI cannot replicate this. It cannot carry consequence. It cannot feel tension. It cannot build intuition grounded in real stakes.

The premium sits here because this layer is where value accumulates, and it is getting scarcer.

Empathy builds loyalty

Empathy is the part most professionals undervalue – and most clients value very highly.

You remember the lawyer who calls back quickly, explains clearly and treats your concerns as legitimate. You remember the one who listens without judgement. You remember the one who keeps you informed, even when the news is uncomfortable. You remember the one who, perhaps, even had to step in and save you from yourself – which, in my case, is far too often.

These behaviours signal safety. They build trust. They determine whether you recommend them, return to them or stay with them.

AI can imitate tone but it cannot earn trust. It cannot take responsibility or hold the weight of someone else's uncertainty.

In this environment, trust becomes the ultimate differentiator, rather than the decoration on top.

What the lawyer test means for leaders

Once you see this pattern with lawyers, it becomes impossible not to see it everywhere else. The logic within this test holds far beyond the legal profession. It applies to every executive, every manager and every organisation facing AI disruption.

The organisations that thrive will be the ones that:

- **Automate the teachable:** These organisations will use AI to compress routine expertise and free capacity for judgement.

- **Accelerate the formation of experience:** They will give their teams earlier exposure to tougher, more varied problems, and so recreate the formative experiences that automation has removed.
- **Design for trust, not just output:** These organisations will track response time, follow-through, clarity and sentiment with rigour. They will treat trust as structural rather than soft.
- **Separate tasks from judgements:** They will measure the quality of decisions, and not simply the volume of activity.

What this test means for customers and teams

Clients expect more speed because AI delivers it elsewhere. They expect clarity because ambiguity has increased. They expect reassurance amid rising volatility.

They want professionals who can translate complexity into options, options into decisions and decisions into outcomes.

Internally, the pattern is similar. Managers who rely on expertise alone will fall behind. Teams that cling to old task-based definitions of competence will struggle as AI absorbs those tasks. The remaining work will be the kind that demands judgement and trust.

The real lesson

The lawyer test is not really about lawyers. It is a mirror for every profession.

It shows where value now lives. It shows why judgement and trust need to rise as expertise becomes abundant. It shows why experience becomes the prized asset in an organisation and why empathy becomes the moat that protects customer loyalty and workforce cohesion.

It shows why, in an AI-saturated world, the work that remains is the work only humans can do.

Playbook: The new professional equation

Here's how you and your team can stay valuable as expertise becomes abundant:

1. **Stop selling knowledge and start selling judgement:** Knowledge is now infrastructure, and clients assume you have it. What they value is how you weigh trade-offs, read context and decide under pressure. Make your judgement visible. Explain how you think, and not just what you know.
2. **Design for exposure, not tenure:** Experience forms through consequence, not time served. Give your team varied, high-stakes problems earlier. Rotate them through unfamiliar contexts. Build the muscle of judgement deliberately rather than hoping it accumulates.
3. **Measure decision quality, not activity:** Activity metrics reward busyness, whereas decision metrics reward discernment. Track the accuracy, speed and impact of judgements. Treat each decision as a learning asset that strengthens experience across the team.
4. **Make trust a design principle:** Trust is not a soft skill. It shapes adoption, loyalty and influence.

Measure it through response time, clarity, follow-through and sentiment. Build systems that reinforce reliability, transparency and ownership.

5. **Balance machine efficiency with human depth:** Let AI remove friction, but never connection. Use it to compress expertise and surface insight. Redirect human effort to conversations, interpretations and relationships where trust is earned and held.

Provocation: The human dividend

AI has handed out knowledge to everyone and sped up mediocrity. That is the uncomfortable truth. When the same information is available to all, expertise stops being an advantage and starts becoming infrastructure. AI narrows the gap between the competent and the merely capable. It raises the floor, not the ceiling.

What still grows is the human component. Experience and empathy remain stubbornly difficult to automate. Judgement built through consequence and trust built through relationship rise in value as the technical layer becomes cheap and abundant. The more AI accelerates expertise, the more it exposes what only humans can deliver.

This is the new professional divide:

- Those who trade in answers will compete with algorithms.
- Those who trade in judgement and trust will earn the premium.

The question for you as a leader is simple but not easy: are you building capability in the layer the machine is taking, or the layer the machine cannot touch? Many organisations are still adding weight to expertise, even as it erodes. Few are investing in the skills that will outlast automation. Fewer still are reshaping roles, pathways and systems to protect the development of judgement and the practice of trust.

The harder truth is this: technology does not decide what gets automated. Leaders do. **Every automation choice you make is also a choice about what humans will still be expected to do.** Remove too much and you hollow out experience. Remove too little and you fall behind. The boundary matters because it defines the future of your workforce.

So before you ask how to make your organisation smarter, ask a sharper question: how much humanity are you willing to automate away?

The future of work will not belong to the people who know the most. It will favour those who make sound decisions and earn enduring trust.

What's next

The new triad of work sets the stage for a tougher question: if value has shifted, how fast is your organisation moving to match it? AI does not just change what work matters. It accelerates every competitive force acting on you and your organisation. Markets move faster. Competitors adapt sooner. Customers expect more. The gap between knowing and deciding becomes the gap between leading and lagging.

In the next chapter, the focus moves from work to people. As AI takes over execution, the human contribution becomes clearer and more exposed. Decisions carry more weight.

Trust becomes more fragile. Imagination becomes more valuable. The challenge is no longer whether your organisation has enough capability, but whether your workforce is designed to support the kinds of judgement, relationships and creativity the new triad now demands.

CHAPTER 2

The human edge

If I am honest, I am more of a *Star Wars* fan than a 'trekkie'. Every now and then, however, I find myself watching the original *Star Trek*, not for the charismatic James T Kirk or the cheesy 1960s special effects but, mostly, for the uniforms.

The shirt colours did something quietly brilliant. They made roles visible. Yellow meant 'command', 'Kirk', 'helm' and 'tactical'. This was the colour worn by the people who made decisions and lived with the consequences. Blue was worn by the science and medical people – including Spock, Dr McCoy and the interpreters. These were the ones who made sense of the unknown and kept everyone alive. And then there were the people who wore the red shirts. They provided security, and were loyal and brave – and usually doomed. If a red shirt beamed down to a planet, you knew how that episode was ending. Ah, the poor red shirts. Ouch.

It was crude and obvious, but it worked. Everyone knew why they were there. Everyone knew what was expected of them.

And everyone knew who to look to when a particular kind of work needed doing.

That idea has always stayed with me. Not the sci-fi roles, but the structure. Humans cluster naturally around craft. We gravitate towards people who practise the same discipline, wrestle with the same problems and speak the same shorthand. This is why guilds keep reappearing in modern organisations – Agile guilds and design guilds; engineering chapters and communities of practice. When people who do similar work come together, they can mentor, develop and hold standards in a way no central HR function ever can.

Real advantages exist here. Skills deepen faster, judgement compounds and identity becomes tied to contribution rather than title. People get better because they are surrounded by others who care about the same work.

And yet, despite knowing all of this, most organisations still design roles as if humans are interchangeable generalists.

The typical management job description is a Frankenstein creation. Make the plan. Execute the plan. Hire the team. Coach the team. Resolve conflict. Create new revenue. Manage risk. Shape culture. Inspire innovation. Deliver results – and preferably all before lunch.

In theory, it sounds admirable. In practice, it is absurd.

While exceptions are possible, it is rare to find people who are genuinely good at every element of that management list. It is even rarer to find people who enjoy all of it. What usually happens instead is compromise. People lean into the parts they are comfortable with and tolerate the rest.

Judgement gets rushed, perhaps, relationship work gets ignored. Creativity gets postponed. The job gets done, but the contribution is less than effective.

Leadership and organisational consultants have been circling this problem for years. We've looked at skills-based work, capability frameworks and strategic workforce planning. We analysed the long, slow death of the job description. We have known for some time that work was drifting away from neat task bundles and static roles. We just never quite forced ourselves to act on it.

AI changes that – not because it introduces new ideas, but because it removes the excuses. When machines take over the doing, what is left becomes impossible to ignore. You can no longer pretend that tasks equal value. You can no longer hide behind activity. You have to confront the uncomfortable truth that different kinds of human work require different kinds of humans.

AI did not invent this problem. It simply pushed it into the open.

At that point, the question stops being abstract and becomes practical. Who in your organisation is here to decide? Who is here to hold trust? Who is here to create the new? And why are they all wearing the same uniform?

That is the edge this chapter is trying to expose. I'm not offering nostalgia for coloured shirts, but clarity of contribution. Because in a world where work is dissolving, roles that mix everything together are not flexible. They are fragile.

And unlike the red shirts, you do not get to blame the script when things go wrong.

When work moves faster than your workforce

Work has changed shape far faster than the systems built to manage it. AI has absorbed the predictable, procedural tasks that once defined jobs. It drafts the first version of almost everything. It performs analysis before a human has opened the file. It coordinates, reports, summarises and packages information without complaint. What remains is the work that carries consequence: the judgement call that shapes a customer outcome, the conversation that protects trust, the interpretation that avoids a strategic misstep, the ethical line that must not be crossed and the imaginative leap that creates new value. Yet the architecture of modern organisations still assumes the opposite world. It assumes tasks equal contribution. It assumes job descriptions define identity. It assumes work is predictable and skills are scarce.

This mismatch has become a structural risk. Organisations are still hiring for skills that AI now performs at scale, overlooking the capabilities that AI cannot replicate. They reward activity instead of judgement. They measure output instead of consequence. They promote based on tenure instead of sense-making. And they design roles as if work moves vertically through a hierarchy when, in reality, intelligent work moves sideways, diagonally and continuously. Expertise has become abundant. Experience has become scarce. Empathy and trust has become fragile. And imagination has become a competitive advantage rather than a creative indulgence.

The cost of this mismatch sneaks up on you. People are busy, but not making a difference. Leaders are awash in information, but clarity is scarce. Careers move faster, but feel emptier. And just as AI raises the stakes, organisations find themselves with the wrong people in the wrong roles, working on the wrong things.

The challenge is clear: rebuild the workforce around the work only humans can do, and create systems that help people grow, get recognised and be measured for those contributions. In this chapter, I introduce two practical tools to help you and your organisation do so: a map of the ten human areas that matter most in an AI-native world, and a blueprint for redesigning roles, hiring, performance and careers to match.

Why now: Work has shifted from doing to deciding

AI has changed the speed, shape and feel of work much faster than organisations have changed how they manage people. For years, companies chased efficiency and predictability. Jobs were a list of tasks, careers were ladders and performance was output. That made sense when work stood still. But now, work is in motion. It's dynamic, distributed and deeply tangled up with AI.

Three big shifts have made the old work playbook obsolete:

1. **AI has collapsed the distance between novice and expert:** As highlighted throughout this book, in almost every field of knowledge, AI can now produce work at a level that once required years of experience. First drafts, baseline analyses, technical scaffolding, initial diagnostics and structured summaries arrive almost instantly. This means the traditional apprenticeship model has inverted. Juniors can produce senior-quality artefacts, but without the judgement that seniors earned through years of exposure.

Experience naturally accumulates through repetition and responsibility. AI removes the repetition while preserving the responsibility. The result is experience scarcity: the work that teaches judgement evaporates, while the decisions requiring judgement remain. Without redesigning how organisations build experience, capability gaps will widen silently until they become visible failures.

2. **Human work has shifted from doing to deciding:** As AI takes over execution, humans inherit consequences. The centre of gravity in work is moving from effort to interpretation, negotiation and sense-making. Most organisations are not built to support this shift. Performance systems reward throughput, not judgement quality. Job architecture still assumes 'more senior = more capability' rather than 'more senior = better decisions under pressure'. Recruitment frameworks prioritise technical skills over the cognitive and emotional range required for intelligent work. And most leaders still see decision quality as an innate personal trait rather than something that can be assessed, developed and measured. The more AI accelerates execution, the more organisations need to rely on humans to slow down, think clearly and handle the parts of work machines should never touch.
3. **Agility now depends on human capability, not structural efficiency:** Organisational agility is no longer about speed of delivery. It is about the speed of learning, and learning is increasingly a human capability problem. AI can surface patterns, generate options and forecast outcomes. But organisations still move at the pace of their slowest moment of human judgement or their deepest pocket of cultural resistance. When structures reward compliance over curiosity, alignment over interpretation or hierarchy

over collaboration, agility dies. The organisation becomes technically advanced but cognitively rigid. In this world, the workforce is either an accelerant or a brake. Without redesigning roles, capabilities and performance around agility, the organisation will continue to know more than it can act on.

Put these shifts together and a single truth emerges: technology is no longer the bottleneck. The real constraint is the shape of the workforce built around it.

AI throws that architecture into sharp relief. It spotlights the gaps between what people know and what the work now needs. It shows where empathy and trust is fragile, where decision rights are fuzzy, where skills miss the mark and where culture digs in its heels. Suddenly, as a leader you can no longer dodge the question: what, exactly, are humans here to do?

The organisations that answer this now will move faster, learn faster and compound value over time. The ones that avoid it will remain trapped in the illusion of progress, busy but brittle, with talent systems optimised for a world that no longer exists.

The framework: Designing the workforce around human contribution

The move from doing to deciding is not just a trend. It is the new backbone of modern work. AI has swept away the predictable, routine tasks, leaving behind the work that carries real human weight: judgement, empathy, trust, ethics, interpretation and imagination. Yet most organisations still act as if tasks are value. That mismatch is why you likely feel anxiety, confusion and misalignment as a leader today.

The frameworks that follow start somewhere new. Instead of building around yesterday's roles, they begin with the work only humans can do. Two models bring this to life. The first maps the ten areas where human contribution still matters most. The second shows how to turn those contributions into real roles, hiring, development and performance.

Together, these models give you and your organisation a way to redesign your workforce – on purpose, with clarity and with confidence – for the age of intelligent work. **AI is not replacing humans, but it is reconfiguring them.** This is how to design for that.

Model one: The Human Contribution Map

The Human Contribution Map, shown in the following figure, points to ten areas where humans still make the biggest difference, even as AI takes over the doing. These ten areas cluster into three domains: decide, relate and create. These are not just skills but also the ways people add value that machines cannot. They show up in every industry and job title, because they mark the human margin: the place where what you can do meets what really matters.

These are the contributions that must stay human if your organisation wants to stay safe, trusted and unique. They are also the places where the strain is felt most, because AI makes the gaps more obvious.

The work that will stay human

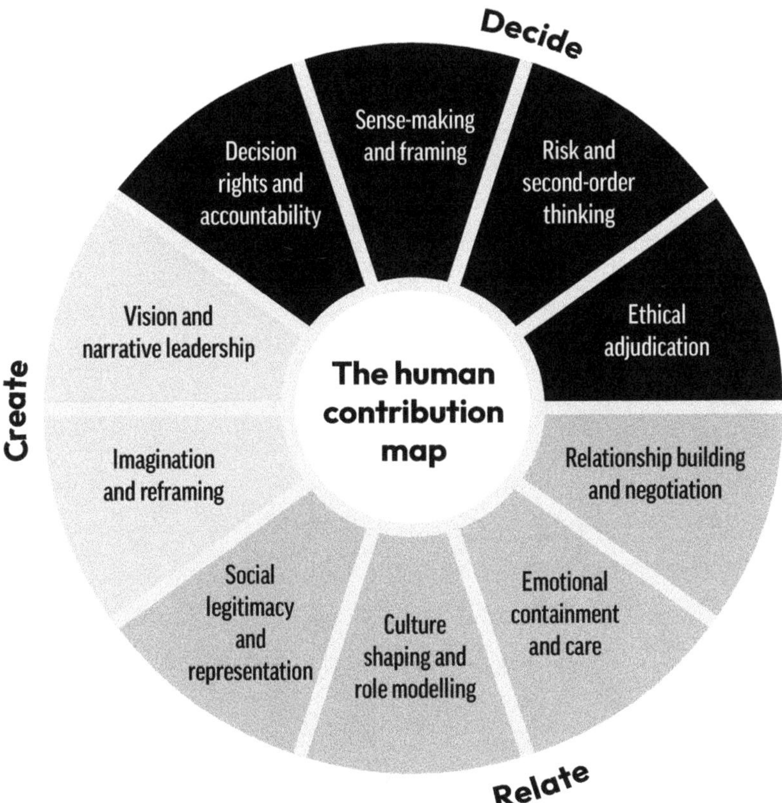

Let's walk through each of the three domains and see why they matter.

The decide domain: Where humans hold consequence

As AI accelerates execution, humans inherit responsibility. The decide domain within the Human Contribution Map includes the four contributions in which judgement shapes outcomes and accountability cannot be delegated. These are:

- **Decision rights and accountability:** AI can generate options, but it cannot own the outcome of a choice. Someone must decide which path to take, shoulder the trade-offs and explain the result. These decisions require moral courage and clarity of intent. Organisations decay when this responsibility is ambiguous.
- **Sense-making and framing:** AI can spot patterns, but it cannot say which ones matter. Framing is a human act: making sense of context, defining the real problem and shaping how others see the landscape. Most strategy fails not because of bad execution, but because of bad framing.
- **Risk and second-order thinking:** AI predicts what happens next. Humans have to think about the ripples of these impacts, including the side effects and long-term impacts that go beyond the model. This means seeing regulatory risk, reputation and hidden fragility. Good risk judgement comes from experience and perspective.
- **Ethical adjudication:** AI optimises. Humans decide what is right. As more decisions are made by algorithms, ethical reasoning becomes an even more important human contribution. It protects trust, safeguards legitimacy and sets the boundaries for automation.

The relate domain: Where humans carry trust

If the decide domain is about consequence, the relate domain is about confidence. The four contributions within this domain shape the organisation's emotional and social fabric.

They cannot be automated, because they depend on presence, empathy and human intuition. They are:

1. **Relationship building and negotiation:** AI cannot build trust. It cannot smooth over tension or mend small cracks between people. As more work is automated, human relationships become the oil that keeps your organisation running smoothly.
2. **Emotional containment and care:** Humans feel fear, hope, pride, confusion, empathy and conflict. AI cannot hold these emotions. If you can absorb emotional swings and respond with steadiness as a leader, you can become an anchor in a fast-moving organisation.
3. **Culture shaping and role modelling:** Culture is what leaders do, not what they say. As work gets more fluid and less structured, role modelling becomes the anchor. People watch for cues from you to figure out what 'good' looks like when the path is unclear.
4. **Social legitimacy and representation:** Customers, regulators and employees still want human accountability when it counts. When something matters, people want to see and hear from a person, not a process.

The create domain: Where humans generate the new

The final domain is about how humans expand the organisation's options, not by repeating what already exists but by imagining what could be. The two contributions within the create domain are as follows:

- **Vision and narrative leadership:** AI can sum up the past. It cannot paint a picture of a future worth chasing. As a leader, you can build belief by telling the story of where your organisation is headed and why it matters.

- **Imagination and reframing:** AI fills in the blanks. Humans reinvent. The ability to challenge assumptions, spot hidden opportunities and reframe stubborn problems is one of the few renewable advantages we have left.

Why the map is the new foundation of workforce design

The Human Contribution Map is both a diagnosis and a design brief. It shows where human capability needs to focus as tasks disappear, apprentice paths shrink and expectations climb. It is also a mirror. When organisations struggle with agility, decision quality, trust or innovation, the root cause is almost always a weakness in one of these ten domains.

The map replaces old ideas of skills matrices with a clearer view of the human edge: the work that is left when AI does everything else.

But just spotting human contribution is not enough. Your organisation needs a way to design roles, assess talent and measure performance around it. That is where the Workforce Blueprint comes in.

Model two: The Workforce Blueprint

If the Human Contribution Map shows what humans are for, the Workforce Blueprint shows how to build a team that can deliver. As highlighted in the following figure, it does this by swapping job descriptions for three core role families: decision leaders, trust builders and value creators. These families are the new operating logic for the human workforce in an AI-native world.

How human contribution becomes organisation capability

	Decision leaders	Trust builders	Value creators
	The stewards of consequence	*The guardians of confidence*	*The architects of the new*
Required capabilities	Pattern recognition Systems thinking Moral reasoning Escalation discipline Information triage Trade-off navigation Signal discernment	Emotional regulation Active listening Boundary setting Conflict navigation Perspective taking Cultural fluency Empathic steadiness	Curiosity Insight synthesis Pattern mixing across domains Creative reasoning Ambiguity tolerance Exploration discipline Story shaping
Core contributions	**Decision rights and accountability** **Sense-making and framing** **Risk and second-order thinking** **Ethical adjudication**	**Relationship building and negotiation** **Emotional containment and care** **Culture shaping and role modelling** **Social legitimacy and representation**	**Vision and narrative leadership** **Imagination and reframing**
Value created	High-quality decisions under uncertainty Clear framing that avoids wasted effort Reduced strategic and operational fragility Decisions aligned with intent and trust	Cohesion under pressure Reduced conflict drag Clearer communication Higher cultural legitimacy Psychological safety	New avenues for growth Clear and aligned future narratives Higher learning velocity Stronger innovation portfolio Strategic resilience

Every role leans towards one of these families. Each family lines up with one of the three contribution domains. Together, they form a structure that matches the real shape of modern work.

Decision leaders: The stewards of consequence

Decision leaders inhabit the decide domain. They are the individuals your organisation relies on when the stakes are high and the information is incomplete. Their work is defined not by tasks but by judgement. They frame the issue, interpret signals, make trade-offs and hold themselves accountable.

These are not always your most senior people, but they are the ones who matter when it counts. What sets them apart is their ability to stay calm under pressure, think clearly and tie decisions back to strategy. They have ethical maturity, systems thinking and pattern recognition.

You cannot measure their performance by output alone. You need hindsight reviews, decision-quality checks, alignment between choices and outcomes, and healthy risk escalation. In an AI-native organisation, decision-making becomes a craft, and decision leaders are its practitioners.

Trust builders: The guardians of confidence

Trust builders anchor the relate domain. They hold together your organisation's emotional and relational infrastructure in a world where workflows and interactions are increasingly automated. As AI handles more of the operational load, the human load becomes more emotional and empathetic.

Trust builders bring steadiness when things get rough. They manage conflict, guide tough conversations, support colleagues through uncertainty and act as quiet cultural stewards.

They are skilled at reading people and situations, and spotting the undercurrents that algorithms miss.

You feel their impact in trust levels, customer sentiment, reputation and how well problems get escalated. Where decision leaders bring clarity, trust builders bring cohesion. They are not a nice-to-have. They are the shock absorbers of the organisation.

Value creators: The architects of the new

Value creators live in the create domain. They expand your organisation's options. They are not just 'innovators' in name, but also the people who challenge assumptions, imagine new paths and mix ideas in fresh ways.

In an AI-native organisation, these roles are essential for staying ahead. AI can remix what already exists, but it cannot create something new. Value creators spot opportunities others miss. They explore, experiment and tell stories that open new paths for growth.

Their contribution becomes visible in your organisation's innovation portfolio, its learning velocity and the new revenue streams or strategic options they generate. They thrive in ambiguity and help the organisation do the same.

Why the blueprint matters now

The Workforce Blueprint solves three systemic problems that legacy people systems cannot.

First, it swaps tasks for contribution as the real unit of work. This matters when tasks vanish into automation and work becomes fluid and contextual.

Second, it fixes the hiring signal problem. Most organisations still hire for technical capability, credentials or experience in work now done by AI. The blueprint shifts hiring towards judgement, EQ and imagination: the capabilities that remain scarce and strategic.

Third, it reframes performance around consequence, not just output. This matters because output is no longer what sets people apart. Now, the quality of decisions, the strength of relationships and the creation of new options are the work.

In combination, the Human Contribution Map and the Workforce Blueprint offer you a practical, durable and strategically aligned way to redesign your workforce for intelligent work. They ensure that as AI accelerates execution, humans accelerate contribution rather than confusion.

This is how your organisation can become truly AI-native: not by automating everything, but by designing the human system that enables intelligent work.

Application: Designing work when job descriptions die

Once you understand what only humans can contribute within your organisation, your next step is execution. This is where most organisations stall. They try to modernise their workforce using tools built for a different era: job descriptions written around tasks, capability frameworks shaped by stability, performance systems optimised for output, and recruitment pipelines focused on technical skills rather than judgement or trust and empathy.

To build a workforce for intelligent work, you and your team need to rethink these systems from the ground up. Not by ripping everything out, but by redesigning the scaffolding that shapes how people are hired, developed and evaluated. The challenge is not headcount. It is architecture. The work has changed. The workforce must catch up.

In the following sections, I outline the practical moves that bring the Human Contribution Map and the Workforce Blueprint to life.

Start by mapping the work, not the roles

You may be tempted to start with your organisational charts. Resist this temptation. Charts describe structure, not work. Begin instead with a contribution audit of the functions that matter most: product, customer operations, finance, risk, engineering, HR, sales and strategy. In essence, you are building a 'work chart' to replace the org chart.

For each functional area, ask three questions:

- Which tasks are already being done by AI or will be within 12 to 18 months?
- Which decisions or moments of trust remain human, and why?
- Where is imagination required to unlock new value or avoid stagnation?

Leaders almost always discover the same pattern: 60 to 80 per cent of activity is execution that should migrate to AI agents, and the remaining 20 to 40 per cent is high-consequence human work distributed unevenly across roles.

This audit is the first real moment of clarity. It shows where human capability is wasted, and where judgement, trust and creativity are being squeezed out by admin overload. Once you see the true shape of work, redesign is the only way forward.

Reclassify roles into the three families

Once the work is mapped, roles can be rebuilt around contribution, not tasks. This is the moment the job description starts to fade away.

Each existing role is evaluated against the Human Contribution Map and assigned a primary orientation:

- decision leader
- trust builder
- value creator.

This does not reduce people to categories but instead reduces confusion. It clarifies where each role's centre of gravity lies, which contribution matters most and what your organisation should expect from the role.

The practical impact is immediate. You start to see which roles need redesigning rather than reskilling. You can recognise that some individuals are sitting in jobs where their natural strengths are underused. And you can notice which parts of your organisation have no-one assigned to essential contributions such as second-order thinking, cultural stewardship or reframing.

This reclassification sets the stage for everything that follows.

Redesign the work so humans do the human parts

Once roles are aligned to contribution, the next step is to redesign the work itself. Most organisations find that decision leaders spend too much time updating slides and chasing information. Trust builders get pulled into operational noise instead of focusing on relationships. Value creators are buried under governance meant for predictable work.

As a leader, you must deliberately clear the space for human contribution to flourish. That means:

- removing administrative drag
- reassigning coordination work to agents
- shifting reporting to automated telemetry
- reducing the number of approvals required for routine decisions
- consolidating low-consequence tasks into automated workflows.

The goal is not efficiency but focus. Every minute a decision leader spends formatting documents is a minute not spent interpreting signals. Every hour a trust builder spends on scheduling is an hour not spent stabilising the team. Every day a value creator spends navigating bureaucracy is a day not spent creating new options.

Redesign gives people back the space to do the work only humans can do.

Rebuild hiring around judgement, trust and imagination

Once roles are clarified and work is redesigned, hiring must be transformed. Traditional job descriptions ask for technical skills, domain expertise and experience with tasks that AI now performs. This results in the wrong people being hired for the wrong work.

Hiring should now be anchored in the Human Contribution Map in the following ways:

- Decision leader hiring needs to focus on decision quality, ethical maturity, pattern recognition, the ability to frame ambiguous situations and the willingness to take accountability. Candidates should be assessed through scenario work, decision logs, case reviews and ambiguity simulation.
- Trust builder hiring should centre on emotional regulation, conflict handling, empathy, negotiation skills and cultural fluency. Assessment should involve role-plays, tension scenarios and feedback interpretation.
- Value creator hiring needs to emphasise curiosity, reframing ability, synthesis across domains and comfort with uncertainty. Candidates should respond to open-ended problems, rapid-prototyping challenges and narrative-building exercises.

Resumes matter much less than what your people have actually contributed. AI-native organisations hire for judgement, not just skill, and for imagination, not just experience.

Reset performance to match the new work

Performance management is one of the most misaligned systems in modern organisations. All too often, it measures speed, volume, accuracy and activity. In an AI-native organisation, these are machine metrics. Humans should be evaluated on something different.

Performance must be rebuilt around contribution:

- Decision leaders should be evaluated by the quality of their decisions, the clarity of their framing, their escalation discipline and the alignment between choices and outcomes.
- Trust builders need to be evaluated by trust and empathy signals, emotional stability under pressure, the health of relationships and the legitimacy they create with customers or employees.
- Value creators should be evaluated by learning velocity, the strength of experiments, the quality of options generated and the value created over time.

These things can be measured through thoughtful design. And they give a much clearer picture of human impact than old KPIs ever could.

Redesign early career pathways before they collapse

One of the quiet crises of knowledge work is the collapse of apprenticeship. Juniors produce high-quality work with AI assistance but get little exposure to the situations that build experience. Without deliberate pathways, experience scarcity could cripple your organisation within years.

Combatting this means redesigning early career development entirely with the following:

- rotations into high-judgement environments
- shadowing of real decision moments
- simulations that replicate conflict, trade-offs and ambiguity
- coaching on sense-making, not just skill acquisition.

Early talent needs to be grown as future decision leaders, trust builders or value creators – not just task doers. This redesign may be the most important investment you can make as a leader.

Institutionalise rhythm, not projects

Finally, your organisational redesign needs rhythm to last. Workforce design in intelligent organisations is not a one-time fix. It is an ongoing cycle.

You need to embed the following in your organisation:

- quarterly contribution reviews
- feedback from AI telemetry into capability development
- regular recalibration of roles as automation increases
- ongoing assessment of judgement, trust and imagination as strategic assets.

This rhythm keeps workforce design from slipping back into old task thinking. It keeps human contribution at the heart of performance.

The payoff: Clarity, coherence and confidence.

When your organisation uses this framework, three things happen fast. People know what their roles are for, not just what they do. Leaders can develop and evaluate talent based on what really matters. And the organisation moves faster, because judgement, trust and imagination finally have room to breathe.

AI speeds up execution. This redesign speeds up contribution. People stop competing with machines and start doing what only humans can.

Playbook: Building a workforce for intelligent work

Here's how to ensure humans are doing what only they can in your organisation:

1. **Redesign roles around contribution, not tasks:** Swap job descriptions for one-page role blueprints that spell out the main contribution: decision leader, trust builder or value creator. Make it clear what the role is for, not just what it does. This one move brings clarity, cuts noise and lines people up with the work only humans can do.
2. **Hire for judgement, trust and imagination:** Shift hiring away from technical experience and towards signs of real contribution. Use scenario cases for decision leaders, tension simulations for trust builders and open-ended challenges for value creators. If a candidate cannot show the contribution, they cannot do the role.
3. **Remove drag so humans can do the human work:** Audit where decision leaders, trust builders and value creators are spending time. Strip out administrative load, automate reporting and shift coordination to agents. Every hour reclaimed becomes higher quality judgement, stronger relationships or better ideas.
4. **Reset performance around consequence:** Stop measuring people on machine metrics such as speed and volume. Evaluate decision leaders on decision

quality, trust builders on empathy and trust signals, and value creators on learning speed and value creation. Performance should match the real work, not the old work.

5. **Protect and accelerate early career experience:** Design modern apprenticeships. Rotate juniors through high-judgement environments, give them real exposure to decisions and use simulations to build experience safely. Without this, the pipeline for future decision leaders, trust builders and value creators dries up.

The provocation: What are humans now for?

AI is already moving the line between effort and consequence. It has taken the work. Now it is revealing the people. Every organisation that leans on smart tools hits the same moment of clarity: they do not have a talent shortage but a design problem.

You have people doing work a machine should do, and machines doing work a human should do. You have job descriptions for a world that is gone. You have performance systems grading tasks that no longer matter. And you have a workforce stretched thin, because your organisation has never stopped to ask the simplest question in the age of AI: what are humans actually here for?

The organisations that thrive will not be those that automate the fastest. They will be the ones that redesign the human system with the same ambition they apply to the technical one. They will protect judgement. They will elevate trust. They will invest in imagination. They will hire, develop and measure people for the work only people can do.

Everything else is just noise.

Your workforce is no longer a map of your organisational hierarchy. It is a map of you and your organisation's ability to navigate uncertainty, take responsibility and create value that AI cannot. And that map is being rewritten whether you lead it or not.

So here is the provocation. If you started from scratch tomorrow, with all the AI you have today, would you rebuild your workforce the way it is now? Or would you design it around the human edge you will need for the next decade?

What's next

Designing the human system clarifies what people are for. But clarity alone does not keep an organisation safe. The harder problem is what happens once AI is embedded deep inside day-to-day operations, quietly doing more and more of the work. As automation accelerates, judgement, experience and trust are no longer tested occasionally – they are tested continuously. Without clear boundaries, efficiency starts to crowd out depth, and capability erodes long before anyone notices. The next chapter shifts the lens from workforce design to automation discipline. Rather than asking how much you can automate, it asks what must remain human if your organisation is to stay credible, resilient and trusted when the system does not behave as expected.

CHAPTER 3

Who's in the cockpit?

Most people who know me know I am a nervous flyer. I might not be the dramatic kind – no white knuckles and no theatrics – but I do have a quiet, persistent awareness that I am voluntarily sitting inside a metal tube moving at a speed that would make my grandmother cross herself.

I have never let this nervousness stop me. I have logged more flights than I care to admit and enough air miles to earn the right to argue with airline loyalty programs on principle. But nervous flyers develop hobbies. Some people do breathwork. I watch air crash investigations.

It is not the crashes that hook me but the discipline. It's the calm voices, and the relentless, almost boring focus on systems, signals and small decisions that compound into outcomes. The phrase I hear again and again in these investigations is not 'the computer failed'. It is 'the system behaved in a way the crew did not expect'.

Modern aviation automation is extraordinary. Most commercial aircraft can taxi, take off and land on autopilot. In some conditions, they can do all of it with astonishing precision. And yet nobody boards a plane and thinks, *Marvellous, we don't have a pilot today.* (At least, nobody I want to share a cabin with.)

Here is the interesting part. We still want a pilot not because we do not trust the technology. We do. We trust it enough to fly thousands of tonnes of humans through the sky, every hour of every day, across weather and oceans and time zones. We trust it because it works most of the time, quietly, and because the industry is obsessive about safety engineering.

But we also know something else. When the system does not behave, the hardest part is not pushing buttons. The hardest part is understanding what is happening, and then making decisions people trust.

That is where *minimum credible expertise* comes in. In a cockpit, expertise is not theoretical but practical. It is the ability to read instruments, sense when a system is drifting, and intervene with competence rather than hope. Even if the autopilot is doing the flying, you want someone up front who can explain what the aircraft is doing without looking at a manual or calling a vendor. You want someone who can challenge the system, not just supervise it.

Then comes *minimum viable experience*. Aviation is one of the few industries that openly admits a truth most organisations try to ignore: judgement is not a certificate. It is accumulation. That is why we talk about flight hours and care about aircraft type ratings. It is also why simulators matter – not because pilots enjoy pretend emergencies, but because experience is how you build pattern recognition under stress. When something fails at

35,000 feet, you do not want that to be the first time your team has had to deal with it.

And then there is *foundational trust*. This is the bit people like to dismiss as 'soft'. But trust is not soft when you are in seat 24C. Autopilot does not have skin in the game. It does not feel consequence. It does not want to get home. A human crew does. They share the same outcome and carry the weight of it. They also know that the cabin is full of nervous humans looking for cues – which is why the pilot's voice on the intercom matters. A calm update does not change the physics of turbulence, but it changes trust. Airlines know this and so do passengers (even the ones pretending not to listen).

A cockpit, in other words, is a neat illustration of what automation gets right when it is disciplined. The automation is powerful, but it sits inside a set of boundaries. It has enough expertise to keep the system credible. But it also has enough experience to respond when the unexpected arrives, and enough human presence to sustain confidence when it gets uncomfortable.

That is the point of what I call the 'automation envelope'. The question you face is not whether you can automate. The question is what you must preserve so your organisation stays safe, capable and believable when the system does not behave.

Because in boardrooms and corridor chats, the story of automation is always the same.

The seduction of AI automation

It's easy to be swept up by the promise of AI-powered automation: more speed, more efficiency and more AI woven into every process. The story is seductive. Let the software handle the complexity. Free your team from the grind. Scale without adding another person. Listen in on any leadership meeting or corridor chat and you'll likely hear automation pitched as the answer to rising costs, scarce talent and mounting operational pressure. The appeal is strong because the logic seems sound. If a task is repeatable, automate it. If a workflow is slow, optimise it. If a team is overloaded, streamline their tasks. Few leaders argue with a chart that shows more output from fewer inputs.

The recent surge in process automation across finance is a good example here. Data entry, reconciliation and reporting used to consume entire teams. Now, much of that work is handled by scripts and AI agents. Human teams move to higher-order tasks. The picture looks neat, modern and rational. It feeds a sense that progress is linear and that every step towards greater automation is a step towards a better organisation. In this context, assuming that more automation is always the right answer is tempting.

But reality rarely behaves. Every wave of technology has carried the same subtle trap. Every innovation encourages leaders to take people out of the loop. The Industrial Revolution replaced skilled craft with mechanised processes. The first spreadsheets changed what finance teams needed to understand. Early automated call centres made customer contact faster, but flattened the empathy and emotional texture that trust depends on. Each tool solved a problem but created a new tension. Progress made businesses more efficient, but also more fragile when things went wrong.

The lesson repeats across decades. **Automation that saves time today can quietly erode the expertise, experience and empathy that made your systems resilient.** The erosion is rarely dramatic. It arrives as a slow fading of the skills and judgement that held everything together. The organisation becomes slicker but shallower. When a system stumbles, the people closest to it no longer know how to recover. The capability gap stays hidden until it is too late.

Automate everything and you don't just cut inefficiency. You also cut away the experience, judgement and learning that your future depends on.

This is the heart of the automation envelope. This envelope is the zone between efficiency and fragility. Stay inside the envelope, and automation amplifies human potential. Step outside, and you risk losing the very things that make your organisation strong. The real question isn't how much you *can* automate, but how much you *should*.

The space between efficiency and fragility

The automation envelope is the discipline that keeps the balance between efficiency and fragility honest. The difference between what can be automated and what should be automated sounds subtle, but it changes everything. Most organisations still treat automation as a technical choice: if the AI is accurate enough and the workflow is stable enough, then automating it feels like progress. But the real cost sits elsewhere. It sits in the experience and judgement you and your team no longer exercise. It sits in the empathy and trust you quietly weaken. In other words, it sits in the human depth you trade away in exchange for short-term efficiency.

The envelope draws a clear line between the value automation creates and the value it erodes. It reminds you as a leader that every automated task removes a moment where people learn, interpret or build the relationships that anchor trust. When these moments disappear across an entire organisation, something important goes missing. Capability decays. Experience thins. Empathy and emotional connection weakens. The organisation becomes efficient but hollow; fast but fragile.

In this chapter, I introduce the three boundaries that define the envelope: minimum credible expertise, minimum viable experience and foundational trust. Together, they describe the lowest acceptable levels of expertise, experience and empathy that must be preserved as you automate. These guardrails are not about slowing progress. They are about protecting the human edge that AI cannot replicate: judgement, trust, interpretation and awareness of consequences.

If you understand these boundaries as a leader, you can avoid the hidden trap of experience scarcity. You can instead strengthen the layers that underpin resilient performance. You can preserve the organisational depth that becomes essential when systems fail or when customers expect more than an automated transaction. The automation envelope is, at its core, a discipline. You can use it to pursue efficiency without compromising the capability, trust and identity that your organisation depends on.

Why now: Automating faster than we are thinking

Automation used to advance in clear, predictable steps. You automated the repetitive tasks, redesigned the workflow and retrained the team. The boundaries were visible. Leaders could see what was being replaced and what would remain.

That clarity has vanished. Generative AI has collapsed the distance between expert work and entry-level work. It no longer automates the fringes. It goes straight for the centre. Reports, analysis, briefings, recommendations and draft decisions are now produced in seconds. The tasks that once built real expertise, experience and judgement are disappearing at the same speed they appear in a prompt window.

This shift matters because pace changes everything. When automation moves slowly, people adapt. They learn new skills. They fill the gaps. They rebuild capability. When automation moves quickly, organisations cannot adjust fast enough. You lose the middle before you realise what the middle meant. Roles become hollowed out. Leaders inherit teams that look experienced on their CVs but haven't developed the judgement that only formative work builds. The organisation becomes efficient but hollow.

The pressure to automate is also rising. Cost curves are tightening. Customers expect instant response and flawless delivery. Boards want proof of productivity. Competitors deploy AI tools, and the temptation is to respond in kind. In many leadership teams, the conversation shifts from whether to automate to how quickly you can automate. The risk is that speed becomes the main factor rather than suitability. Leaders end up solving the wrong problem because they feel the heat before they see the consequences.

Empathy and trust add another layer. Customers have become more sensitive to how organisations automate. They notice when the experience flattens or when real conversations disappear. They worry about errors they cannot trace and decisions they cannot challenge. Automation without boundaries amplifies this anxiety. Trust erodes quietly and restores slowly. Once lost, trust becomes a structural disadvantage rather than a tactical inconvenience.

The workforce is changing too. Entry-level roles have already thinned out. Junior staff are hired into teams where much of the foundational work is automated from day one. They appear competent because AI fills the gaps, but they lack the durability that comes from grappling with real problems. Leaders discover the gap only when they need someone who can act, decide or interpret without an AI model holding their hand. By then, it is too late. Experience cannot be retrofitted.

This is why the automation envelope matters now. The speed, scope and subtlety of generative AI make uncontrolled automation a strategic risk, not a technical one. The envelope provides a way to stay in control. **As a leader, you can use the automation envelope to match automation to capability rather than convenience.** It restores discipline to decisions that have become too easy and too fast. It ensures your organisation gains efficiency without sacrificing depth, judgement or trust. In a world where automation accelerates by default, boundaries become a source of strength.

The framework: The automation envelope

The automation envelope is the structure that keeps automation honest. It defines the space where automation strengthens your organisation rather than weakening its human depth. As shown in the following figure, the framework rests on three guardrails: minimum credible expertise, minimum viable experience and foundational trust. Together, they create the boundaries leaders need to ensure automation never drops the organisation below the human depth it requires.

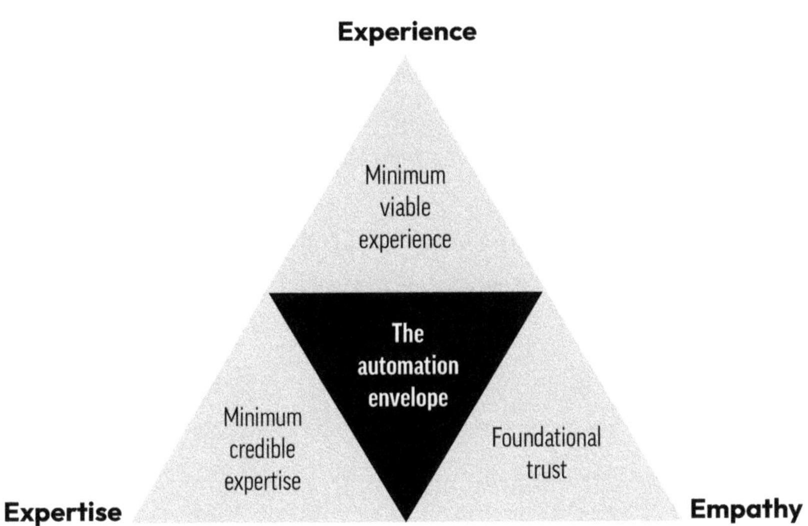

Remember: the envelope exists because automation creates tension. It promises efficiency, but efficiency without judgement becomes brittle. It promises consistency, but consistency without experience becomes shallow. It promises scale, but scale without empathy becomes hollow. The envelope ensures these promises do not turn into risks.

It helps you find a way to progress at pace without stepping into the trap of capability erosion. It keeps your focus on balance rather than speed. And it forces you to consider not just what automation does but also what it displaces.

Guardrail one: Minimum credible expertise

The guardrail of minimum credible expertise sets the floor for your automation envelope. It defines the lowest acceptable level of human expertise that must remain in the system for it to stay safe, adaptable and believable. Even when AI can perform most of the work, you still need enough people who understand the underlying mechanics, can challenge the output and can recover the system when it falters. From my aviation example at the start of this chapter, this is the equivalent of still having a pilot on board who can fly the aircraft, monitor the automation and evaluate whether the systems are behaving as expected.

Signals of a weakening expertise floor tend to appear quietly. Critical processes reach a point where nobody can explain them without referring to the tool. Teams find themselves dependent on a vendor or a lone specialist to interpret incidents. Documentation begins to replace lived understanding in decisions that once required real judgement. Small anomalies take longer to diagnose because nobody has ever encountered the underlying work themselves. This is why airlines still require pilots to complete a minimum number of manual take-offs and landings each year, even though automation can handle them, because expertise that is not exercised eventually stops being credible.

Minimum credible expertise prevents you from stripping out so much knowledge that your organisation can no longer understand, question or safely operate what it has automated.

Guardrail two: Minimum viable experience

Minimum viable experience protects your organisation's experience base. It ensures you and your team maintain sufficient real contact with the work for you to build judgement, recognise patterns and make sound decisions. Without this contact, capability becomes something that looks convincing on the surface but collapses under strain.

Experience is not built through documentation or training modules. It is built through friction, variation and repetition. It comes from resolving edge cases, navigating ambiguity and feeling the weight of choices when the outcome is uncertain. This is why pilots are not certified on an aircraft type until they have logged a minimum number of hours on that specific aircraft, supported by intensive simulator training that rehearses rare but catastrophic failures. The aim is not familiarity with the controls, but judgement formed through exposure.

When automation absorbs these formative moments, the pipeline that develops future judgement and decision-making quietly erodes. Junior staff might appear capable because AI fills the gaps, but the underlying depth becomes thin and brittle. Even experienced pilots are subject to regular check flights and recurrent simulator assessments, precisely because experience that is not refreshed degrades faster than most people expect. Organisations are no different.

Minimum viable experience keeps that talent pipeline intact. It preserves deliberate opportunities for humans to interpret, decide and understand the work beneath the workflow. It prevents your organisation from drifting into a structure where senior leaders carry responsibility without the depth of experience required to exercise it. When minimum viable experience holds, judgement strengthens. When it slips, experience scarcity spreads faster than most leaders expect.

Guardrail three: Foundational trust

Foundational trust safeguards the emotional backbone of your organisation. It establishes the level of human presence required to maintain confidence among employees and customers, especially as automation takes on more of the visible work. Without this anchor, the organisation risks becoming efficient in form but hollow in feeling. In aviation, this is why passengers still expect to hear a human voice from the cockpit, even on a routine flight that is largely flown by automation.

Empathy and trust rarely collapse in a single moment. Trust degrades slowly when interactions feel fake or impersonal, when customers cannot challenge automated decisions, when teams sense they are being replaced rather than supported, and when accountability becomes blurred. **Each small shift seems trivial on its own, yet together they weaken the relational fabric that holds the organisation together.**

Foundational trust prevents this erosion by ensuring automation never overwhelms the human signals that convey competence, care and reliability. It preserves the parts of the experience that earn loyalty and legitimacy. It preserves empathy within your organisation. No autopilot can reassure passengers during turbulence; trust is built through visible human presence and responsibility. Trust takes time to build and even longer to restore. Foundational empathy exists to stop it slipping in the first place.

How the guardrails work together

Minimum credible expertise, minimum viable experience and foundational trust do not operate as separate elements. They behave as a single system that stabilises your organisation's underlying capability, decision quality and resilience under pressure. When automation stretches beyond what people truly understand, minimum credible expertise thins first. Expertise becomes procedural rather than grounded. As expertise weakens, minimum viable experience drops next, because people no longer have enough exposure to build judgement. And when judgement fades, foundational trust erodes, as customers and employees lose confidence in decisions they cannot trace and interactions that no longer feel anchored in human competence and care.

The moment trust begins to slip, the organisation's tolerance for automation contracts. Even highly efficient systems feel risky when people no longer believe anyone can step in if something goes wrong. This creates a feedback loop: weaker expertise undermines experience, weaker experience undermines empathy and trust, and weaker trust reduces the safe use of automation. The envelope exists to interrupt this loop. It forces you to think in interdependencies rather than isolated levers, keeping human capability and care visible at the exact point where technology can easily overshadow it.

Remember experience scarcity: The hidden cost of over-automation

Experience scarcity is not a silent cost so much as a deferred one. It does not appear at the moment automation expands but emerges later, often under pressure, when your organisation realises it has lost more than it intended. Early signals are reassuring rather than alarming: smoother workflows, fewer escalations and faster throughput. Everything appears to be working better.

Where experience scarcity takes hold is across the connective tissue of the organisation, not just at the entry level. As AI absorbs more complexity, fewer people encounter unfamiliar situations. Edge cases are resolved upstream. Exceptions are filtered out. The situation is similar to that in a hospital where junior doctors increasingly rely on diagnostic systems and protocols. Exposure to messy, ambiguous cases becomes rarer, not because illness has disappeared, but because the system shields them from it.

The surface picture still looks strong. Junior staff sound fluent and confident, supported by AI recommendations. Mid-level managers coordinate outputs they have never personally produced. Senior leaders see efficiency gains and assume capability is increasing. In medicine, this is the registrar who has followed hundreds of protocol-driven diagnoses but has rarely had to reason from first principles at three in the morning, with incomplete information and a deteriorating patient. What forms instead is a competence that performs well in stable conditions but has never been stress-tested.

Experience scarcity becomes visible only when conditions change – when a case does not fit the model, for example, or a rare complication appears. A decision must be made without a clear guideline. In those moments, organisations discover that judgement cannot be conjured on demand. Leaders look around and realise they have capable professionals, but too few who have lived through comparable failure before.

This is why minimum viable experience matters. It ensures organisations continue to produce people who accumulate judgement through real exposure, not just supervised output. Without it, capability does not disappear loudly. It thins quietly and then fails suddenly, leaving the organisation efficient and impressive on paper, but unexpectedly fragile under pressure.

How leaders use and interpret the envelope

The automation envelope changes the questions you ask as a leader. Instead of debating accuracy rates or workflow stability, you can start to ask what expertise is weakening, what judgement is being displaced and which experiences your organisation will wish it had preserved. These questions surface risks that never appear in dashboards. They reveal where automation is running ahead of capability and where resilience is quietly thinning behind the scenes.

This line of inquiry also brings clarity to what must be protected. Minimum credible expertise highlights the areas where expertise must remain strong and demonstrable rather than inferred from AI output. Minimum viable experience shows where exposure must be deliberately retained so judgement and decision quality continue to grow rather than atrophy. Foundational trust identifies the moments where human presence is essential to maintain confidence, legitimacy and accountability. When applied together, these guardrails turn automation into a strategic choice rather than a reflex.

Two measures make this discipline practical:

- **Experience coverage ratio:** This shows how much of the work is still touched by people who possess meaningful expertise and have engaged with the underlying complexity.
- **Automation return on experience:** This adjusts efficiency gains for any erosion in capability or trust.

Used consistently, they expose the early signs of fragility: slower crisis response, rising exceptions, hesitant decision-making and customer interactions that feel depersonalised. They turn small signals into strategic warnings and keep leaders honest about whether automation is strengthening or thinning the organisation's depth.

The leadership discipline and strategic value of the envelope

The automation envelope only works when automation decisions are shaped by both technical understanding and human judgement. As a leader, you need people who understand the rhythms, anomalies and tacit knowledge embedded in the work, not just those who understand the models. You must protect the parts of the system that still teach, rather than smoothing them away for the sake of speed. This requires restraint. It demands clarity about which experiences matter in the long term, which expertise must remain credible and where empathy needs active reinforcement. It forces you to resist the instinct to strip away every inefficiency and instead defend the exposures that build depth, adaptability and confidence.

Staying inside the envelope preserves the human foundations that make your organisation resilient. It protects expertise that must be exercised without a model, judgement that strengthens through meaningful exposure and experience, and trust that compounds through empathy and reliable human presence. These qualities cannot be automated. They form the backbone of organisational capability and matter most when systems fail or when customers demand more than transactional efficiency. **In a world where automation accelerates by default, the organisations that thrive will not be those that automate most aggressively, but those that automate with precision, protecting depth with as much intent as they pursue speed.**

The automation envelope keeps that balance intact and ensures progress does not cost your organisation the very abilities that make it strong.

Application: Making the envelope work day to day

Using the automation envelope begins with a shift in how you understand the work itself. Automation is not simply a collection of tools or workflows. It is a chain of decisions about where expertise is exercised, where judgement is built and where trust is reinforced. The envelope makes these decisions visible. It turns abstract boundaries into day-to-day leadership behaviour.

Mapping where automation has crept in

Most organisations automate far more than they recognise. Models draft documents. Agents triage inboxes. Workflow platforms orchestrate processes that previously required human interpretation. Employees quietly lean on AI to complete tasks that once required judgement. Each micro-automation appears harmless, yet together they can hollow out capability before anyone sees the decline.

A practical starting point is to trace a few critical workflows end-to-end. Map where AI now carries the load. Look for tasks that once required grappling with ambiguity, nuance or incomplete information. These moments often disappear quietly, but they are the moments that build depth. When they vanish, the erosion only becomes visible under stress.

Finding the judgement-intensive moments

Every workflow contains moments in which decisions are made under uncertainty. These are the points where trade-offs are weighed, incomplete signals are interpreted and priorities are set. They matter because they determine outcomes, not just efficiency. They define who decides, on what basis and with what consequences.

Automation can reproduce an outcome, but it cannot improve judgement. When systems fully absorb these decisions, the organisation loses visibility into why choices were made, how they could be improved and what data would have strengthened them. As a leader, you must deliberately protect these moments so judgement continues to develop, accountability remains clear and decision quality improves over time. These moments form the backbone of minimum viable experience.

Applying the guardrails

Once the critical moments are visible, leaders can review them against each element.

Start with minimum credible expertise. Identify where the organisation still needs humans with genuine, demonstrable understanding of the work, not proxy expertise inferred from AI-generated output. This often becomes most visible in customer-facing scenarios, exception handling and ambiguous decisions. When the knowledge beneath the workflow weakens, errors increase, confidence dips and differentiation fades.

Then examine minimum viable experience. If formative tasks that build judgement have been automated away, the organisation must reintroduce human exposure. This can feel inefficient in the short term, but it is the only way to maintain a capability base that can act independently of the model.

Finally, consider foundational trust. This erodes when automation feels opaque, lacking in empathy or unaccountable. Early signs show up in tone: customers questioning decisions they cannot challenge, staff hesitating to override automated output or teams feeling displaced rather than supported. These are structural signals, not sentiment.

Operationalising the envelope

Once the guardrails are understood, you must embed them into everyday practice with your team.

Teams need clarity on three questions:

1. Which tasks must remain human-led because they build or exercise judgement?
2. Where is automation welcome and intentional?
3. Where is speed deliberately limited because capability still needs to deepen?

Without this clarity, boundaries look inconsistent. With it, the automation envelope becomes shared practice rather than an abstract principle.

Once established, the envelope also shapes hiring and development in the following ways:

- Ensuring minimum credible expertise means building skill depth, not just workflow familiarity.
- Preserving minimum viable experience means creating exposure pathways for early-career staff.
- Protecting foundational trust means designing roles with relational responsibility rather than removing all human contact.

Experience scarcity often appears here first. If automation has absorbed formative work, hiring alone will not close the gap. Judgement cannot be recruited. It must be built. That means designing roles, rotations and opportunities that expose people to the work beneath the workflow. It means protecting the messy parts of the system that still teach. It means accepting that some inefficiency today is the price of capability tomorrow.

Keeping the envelope alive

The automation envelope is not static. It needs rhythm. Quarterly reviews keep the boundaries aligned with technology shifts, customer expectations and workforce capability. They help you adjust as a leader before the consequences become structural.

Over time, the envelope becomes part of your organisation's operating fabric. It shapes automation priorities, capability investments, customer experience design and your organisation's appetite for speed. It sits underneath strategy rather than beside it.

What the envelope delivers

Applied consistently, the automation envelope provides something essential: it gives you the confidence to automate boldly without hollowing out expertise, judgement or trust. It turns automation from a race into a discipline. It enables:

- speed without fragility
- efficiency without hollowness
- progress without regret.

This is the difference between automation that accelerates the organisation and automation that quietly weakens it.

The envelope keeps you and your organisation on the right side of that line.

Playbook: Setting the boundaries that protect your edge

Here's how to build your automation envelope and put it into practice:

1. **Map your exposure:** Trace critical workflows and identify where AI has already replaced hands-on work. Highlight the judgement moments that are disappearing. These are your capability anchors.
2. **Set your three boundaries clearly:** Define your thresholds in plain language. Decide where expertise must remain credible and human, where experience must be deliberately maintained and where trust requires visible human presence. Make these limits explicit so automation does not drift past them by default.
3. **Design for experience, not just efficiency:** Create deliberate opportunities for exposure to situations that develop experience: rotations, shadowing and controlled friction. Strengthen minimum viable experience by protecting the work that builds judgement. The inefficiencies you preserve today become resilience assets tomorrow.
4. **Make the envelope measurable:** Track the experience coverage ratio and automation return on experience quarterly. Watch for early behavioural

signals such as rising exceptions, hesitation in decision-making or shifts in customer tone. These indicators reveal whether automation is strengthening or weakening your capability.

5. **Embed the envelope in your operating rhythm:** Revisit the boundaries every 90 days. Adjust as technology evolves and the organisation learns. Make the envelope part of your planning, hiring and customer experience. When the boundaries are alive, automation becomes a disciplined advantage, and not a structural risk.

Provocation: AI will expose your strategic gaps

Most organisations will not realise they have exceeded their automation envelope until something breaks. A customer escalation that should have been simple drags into a week of confusion. A junior team that looked capable on paper freezes the moment the AI model offers an answer they cannot interpret. A routine incident turns into a crisis because nobody has the depth to improvise. The automation worked. The organisation did not.

The uncomfortable truth is that organisations rarely notice when they begin to hollow out. What starts as convenience becomes reliance, and reliance eventually exposes fragility. Leaders celebrate efficiency gains while expertise thins, experience drains away and empathy and trust slips beneath the surface. By the time the symptoms appear, the gap is structural, not tactical.

The real risk is not aggressive automation. It is mindless automation. It is the accumulation of small, reasonable decisions that hollow out minimum credible expertise. It is the slow removal of formative work that sustains minimum viable experience. It is the assumption that trust will hold even when human presence has been thinned to the point of invisibility. Capability does not survive in a vacuum. Trust does not recover on command. Experience cannot be rebuilt overnight.

So the provocation is simple. What happens if your next strategic inflection point arrives at the exact moment your organisation carries the least expertise, the weakest relationships and the shallowest experience it has ever held? AI will not close that gap. It will magnify it.

Leaders who treat automation as a race will gain speed and lose resilience. Leaders who treat it as a discipline will gain both. The difference is not the tools. It is the boundaries.

Now is the moment to draw those boundaries with intent. You need to decide what must remain human in your organisation because it builds capability, protect the experiences that your future depends on and reinforce trust when automation pushes it to the edge.

Automation will not slow down. Your restraint is the advantage.

What's next

The automation envelope gives you the boundaries, but boundaries alone do not tell you when to move. The harder problem is timing. AI does not just change what is safe to automate. It also collapses the time leaders have to notice, interpret and respond before advantage erodes. Strategy is no longer a question of direction alone, but of velocity. Markets heat up quietly. Cost structures reset without warning. Customer expectations move before internal cycles can catch up. In the next chapter, the focus shifts from control to speed. It introduces a way to diagnose how fast disruption is burning through your assumptions, and how to recalibrate your decision rhythm before the platform beneath you starts to give way.

CHAPTER 4

Shift happens

Over the course of my almost 30-year executive and consulting career, I have had the privilege of working with and leading inside some remarkable companies. My mum would say this long list is because I cannot hold down a job. I prefer to think of it as a rich tapestry of experience. That experience runs from the early days of the commercial internet at Cisco Systems, through open-source pioneers such as Red Hat, to the rise of software as a service at Salesforce.com, and later roles as the Australian CEO of realestate.com.au and a partner at Deloitte Digital.

A particular thread runs consistently through all of those roles (apart from the occasional abrupt exit). Most of these organisations were doing the disrupting, rather than receiving it. They did not slowly improve existing models. They changed the rules. They moved faster than competitors thought possible, reshaped customer expectations and quietly made once-dominant incumbents irrelevant.

What often surprised me was not how effective these disruptors were; rather, it was how invisible the disruption often felt to everyone else. From the inside, the shift never looked dramatic. No single moment stood out when a market clearly broke. Instead, competitors carried on, confident in their position, their scale and their past success. They did not ignore change. They simply underestimated its speed. By the time they recognised what was happening, their customers had already moved, their cost base no longer worked and their options had narrowed to defensive moves.

Many of those companies no longer exist. Others survive only as shadows of what they once were, absorbed by stronger, newer players. They did not fail because they were foolish or complacent. They failed because they misjudged timing. The water warmed gradually, their organisations adapted just enough to stay comfortable and by the time the temperature became obvious, it was already too late to jump.

This chapter draws on what I learned working inside the companies that did the disrupting. I don't mean the slogans or the innovation theatre, but the underlying patterns that allowed them to move early while others hesitated. The lesson is simple but uncomfortable. Disruption rarely announces itself. It arrives quietly, accelerates invisibly and only looks obvious in hindsight. The leaders who survive are not the smartest in the room. They are the ones who notice the temperature changing before everyone else does.

While every leader likes to believe they would notice the early signs of disruption, most only recognise the shift once it's too late. The awkward part is that everyone assumes they are the exception. Nobody imagines their decisions will one day be dissected in a consulting slide deck as the cautionary tale of a company that missed what was plainly in front of them. Yet in the age of AI, the question is no longer whether disruption is coming. The question is how quickly.

Some organisations are already running on borrowed time. The structural weaknesses have been compounding for years, sustained by legacy systems, slow governance and blind assumptions about customer loyalty. Others show no outward signs of distress, yet the internal indicators point to momentum moving against them. And a few still treat AI as a distant thought experiment, setting up task forces to study the obvious while competitors move ahead with live deployments.

This is the illusion of time. In previous disruptive waves, as a leader you might have had the luxury of patience. You could watch early adopters stumble, convene a steering committee and only move once the risk seemed low. It was always a risky strategy, but that playbook is useless now. AI collapses time in ways that senior executives still underestimate. I have worked in disruptive innovation for three decades, and I have never seen a technology move this fast. What once took a decade to mature now happens in a quarter. A single new model release can reset your cost structures, customer expectations and internal definitions of productivity before your next board pack is produced.

That is why 'wait-and-see' is no longer a strategy. It is professional procrastination dressed up as governance. This is not a bubble. This is not a drill. The pace of change is structural, not cyclical, and pretending otherwise only accelerates the burn.

Meanwhile, the competitive landscape has changed. Rivals you once dismissed as mid-tier distractions now automate half their cost base. Partners you depend on quietly accumulate power as their models become the rails your business runs on. Customers who once tolerated friction now expect instant clarity, personalisation and empathy as standard. The bar has lifted everywhere, all at once.

The real threat is not the disruption outside your organisation. It is the friction inside it. Slow decisions, limited curiosity, poor governance and cultural denial provide the oxygen. Leaders feel busy, but the organisation is not moving. And in an AI-driven world, this friction creates a burning platform.

You have less time than you think.

For many executive teams, this time compression does not feel dramatic. It feels like a subtle but persistent sense of being slightly late to everything. Board papers are always one cycle behind the conversation in the market. Risk papers describe issues that frontline teams have already normalised. Technology decisions arrive neatly formatted for approval long after the options have actually expired. The organisation is always moving, but mostly one beat behind. That is what a burning platform feels like from the inside: busy, serious, committed and quietly out of sync.

The hidden clock behind AI disruption

AI has changed the basis of competition. The sources of advantage that once felt durable now decay the moment a new model enters the market. Expertise, long treated as the cornerstone of value, has become abundant. Every organisation can access similar tools, similar models and similar baseline capability. The differentiator is no longer what you know, but how quickly you can use your experience to interpret signals, make decisions and adapt before the next release resets the field. **Disruption has shifted from a technology problem to a timing problem.**

In this chapter, I outline a practical way for you as a leader to measure that timing. I position disruption as a burn rate you can diagnose, rather than a threat you must fear. Instead of hype cycles, innovation theatre or abstract futurism, I focus on the five competitive forces that reveal how quickly your advantage is eroding: competition, new entrants, substitutes, suppliers and customers. These forces have always shaped markets. AI accelerates them, amplifies them and makes them interact with a volatility that overwhelms slow governance and traditional planning cycles.

My goal is not to generate anxiety. It is to restore clarity. Once you can see your rate of change, you can calibrate your response. If you can understand your disruptive burn rate, you can act earlier, place smarter bets and avoid the inertia that traps incumbents. You can move before competitors automate, before substitutes become acceptable and before customers shift their expectations. And you can accept that denial only accelerates the burn.

This chapter shows you where to look, what to measure and how to separate signal from noise. It helps you spot the heat while the structure is still intact. The aim is to give you a reliable way to understand whether your platform is warming, smouldering or already burning, and what to do next while you still have time to choose rather than react.

Why now: The forces accelerating your burn rate

AI has arrived at a moment when organisations can least afford it. The competitive environment was already tightening through globalisation, digital advances and rising customer expectations. AI compounds these pressures and accelerates every underlying force. Markets move faster. Cost structures shift overnight. Expectations change before leaders can react. The tempo has changed, and organisations built for predictability now face the steepest hill to climb.

Strategy cycles have collapsed

Most organisations still work to annual strategy rhythms. AI moves in monthly ones. A new model release can render a product uncompetitive or an internal process redundant before the next budgeting round. The result is a widening timing mismatch. Leaders believe they are operating prudently. In reality, they are lagging because external change has outpaced internal cadence. You cannot win when you are running at a different speed.

Experience pathways are eroding

AI has automated much of the work that once built expertise and helped develop early-career judgement. Analysts, consultants and project managers used to spend years acquiring the pattern recognition that later informed critical decisions. Those repetitions have vanished. The pool of people with real decision-making depth is shrinking even as decisions become more complex. This is experience scarcity. As a leader, it constrains your organisation's ability to act quickly because fewer people can confidently interpret ambiguous signals.

Supplier power has intensified

AI infrastructure is consolidating around a small number of platforms. Your cost base, innovation velocity and even your ethics footprint increasingly depend on upstream providers. This reverses the historical dependency dynamic. Your risk is no longer losing a supplier. It is the supplier changing terms, models or priorities in ways that immediately reshape your economics. AI technologies that are currently being sold to you as a loss leader may swiftly change pricing after you have embedded them in your business. Power used to shift gradually. Now it shifts instantly. My prediction is your AI bill will soon be your biggest expense item.

When expectations travel faster than strategy

Customer expectations have reset. This isn't because organisations suddenly became worse, but because people experienced something better elsewhere. The most powerful shifts in expectation rarely start at work. They start in everyday life. Amazon trained people to expect instant availability and transparent pricing. Uber taught them to expect real-time updates and frictionless service. Netflix normalised personalisation without effort. Once people experience these standards as consumers, they carry them with them into every other context, including their professional lives.

AI has accelerated this bleed-through. Instant responses, tailored recommendations and high accuracy now feel normal, not exceptional. Customers no longer separate their expectations of a consumer platform from their expectations of a business provider. They compare your organisation to the best experience they have had anywhere, not to the median performer in your industry. When organisations fail to meet this new baseline, they do not look stable or prudent. They look slow, opaque or indifferent, even if their underlying service has not declined at all. The gap is not one of performance deterioration. It is an expectation lift, and it is both relentless and unforgiving.

Organisational culture has slowed

Boards want proof before investment. Executives want guarantees before action. Middle managers want clarity before they change. AI offers none of these. It only offers momentum. This creates cultural drag that compounds every structural weakness. The organisation feels busy, but its metabolism is slow. Activity increases, yet progress stalls.

You can usually hear this cultural drag long before you can see it in the numbers. Executives talk about AI in future tense while their teams already use it in the shadows. Risk functions frame every experiment as a potential breach rather than a source of learning. Finance demands business cases that assume stability in a landscape defined by volatility. None of these behaviours is malicious. They are simply relics of a slower world. The problem is that they compound. Every cautious meeting, every deferred decision, every extra step in the process adds a thin layer of delay. Eventually, those layers form a barrier that even the best strategy cannot push through in time.

As a leader, you do not need perfect foresight. You need a clear view of these accelerating forces and a way to interpret the heat before the structure gives way. Timing has become the new strategic advantage. Faster understanding creates faster adaptation. And faster adaptation is the only way to stay ahead when the platform beneath you is already warming.

The framework: The AI Disruption Velocity Index

Disruption has always been uncomfortable. AI makes it immediate. The challenge for leaders is not predicting the future, but understanding the present with enough clarity to act before the next shift arrives. That is the purpose of the AI Disruption Velocity Index (DVI). It gives you a simple, behavioural diagnostic to assess how quickly pressure is building around your business model. Instead of being left with a feeling of abstract anxiety, you get a structured way to interpret heat, identify patterns and make timing decisions with confidence.

The DVI is built around the five competitive forces already reshaping every sector: competition, new entrants, substitutes, suppliers and customers. These forces are not new, but AI changes their speed and scale. The result is a new form of competitive chemistry. Heat accumulates faster, spreads further and catches leaders off guard unless they have a disciplined way to measure it.

The DVI does not attempt to forecast technology. It does not require a PhD in machine learning. Instead, it draws your attention to where advantage is eroding, where risk is concentrating and where urgency is warranted. You can think of it as a heat map for your organisation. Each component reveals a different source of acceleration. Put them together and you see how quickly your platform is burning.

What matters most is not the score but the pattern. High velocity in one dimension is uncomfortable. High velocity across all five is existential. The leaders who navigate AI disruption effectively are not the ones with the most technical knowledge. They are the ones who sense change quickly, interpret it accurately and adjust their operating rhythm before competitors even realise the market has turned.

The DVI gives you that sensing mechanism.

In practical terms, the DVI is best used as a structured conversation, rather than a spreadsheet exercise. The numbers matter less than the discussion that produces them. Your aim is not to produce a neat index for the board pack but to surface uncomfortable truths. When leaders walk through each force together and ground their scores in specific examples, three things happen. Assumptions become visible. Blind spots become debatable. And the organisation begins to build a shared map of where reality is moving faster than its internal story. That shared map is far more valuable than any single score.

To aid in this discussion, in the following outline of each of the competitive forces I've included reality-check questions to surface assumption and blind spots, and the metrics to focus on.

Competitive acceleration

Competition has always shaped strategy, but AI changes the gradient. Your rivals no longer need large teams, complex systems or deep expertise to outperform you. They need access to the right models and the willingness to deploy them. This collapses cost structures and resets productivity benchmarks. A competitor who can produce the same work at half the cost, twice the speed and with consistent quality does not need a marketing campaign to take your customers. They only need to exist.

Reality-check questions

- How frequently are competitors introducing new capabilities, service improvements or delivery enhancements, and how does this compare to your own pace over the past 6 to 12 months?
- Are competitors reducing turnaround times, improving accuracy or increasing personalisation in ways your organisation cannot currently match?
- Have rivals achieved step-change reductions in cost-to-serve, error rates or fulfilment time through AI, automation or workflow redesign?
- Are competitors winning customers by offering a noticeably smoother, faster or more intelligent end-to-end experience, even without increasing headcount?
- Have you lost tenders, clients or market share because a competitor's operating model is now structurally more efficient or adaptive than yours?

Metrics that matter

- **Pace of improvement:** Frequency of observable service, experience or operational improvements achieved by you versus competitors per quarter.
- **Relative cycle time:** Comparative turnaround time, fulfilment speed or service responsiveness against key competitors.
- **AI-driven efficiency:** Evidence of margin expansion, cost reduction or productivity uplift among competitors versus your baseline.

The new economics of entrants

AI reduces the cost of entry for many industries to almost nothing. In previous eras, new entrants needed capital, talent and time. Today, they need an idea, a model and an internet connection. This does not mean every startup is a threat. It means the barriers you relied on are no longer barriers. Assumptions about the difficulty of competing with you may no longer hold.

Startups were always a concern for incumbents, but they rarely presented an existential threat. They could be monitored, outspent, acquired or outlasted. Most lacked the scale, credibility or operational maturity to pose an immediate risk. AI changes that. New entrants no longer need to grow into competitiveness. They can arrive already efficient, already automated and already operating at a cost base incumbents cannot easily match. What was once manageable disruption has become a direct and immediate threat to established business models.

Reality-check questions

- Could a three-person team replicate at least 60 to 80 per cent of your core value proposition using public AI models, automation platforms or no-code tools?
- Are newcomers entering your category with cost bases that are structurally lower than yours, even though their capabilities are still maturing?
- Are adjacent-industry players beginning to overlap with or encroach on your value chain using AI?
- Are customers building their own lightweight tools or workflows that bypass parts of your product or service?

- If a motivated founder with no sector expertise wanted to compete with you, what real barriers would stop them in the first six months?

Metrics that matter

- **Time-to-replicate:** Estimated weeks required for a small team to build a minimum viable product (MVP) of your major offerings using commercial AI tools.
- **DIY customer workarounds:** Volume of customers self-solving or building their own tools to replace elements of your service.
- **New entrant density:** Number of net-new products, startups or category-adjacent offerings launched in the past 12 months.

Substitute speed

Substitutes used to take decades to gain traction. AI collapses that timeframe. A substitute does not need to be perfect. It only needs to be acceptable. When a cheaper, faster or more convenient alternative becomes instantly available, customers experiment. Once they do, their expectations reset. By the time you notice, the definition of value has already shifted.

Reality-check questions

- What proportion of your core offer can customers now replicate using readily available AI tools or low-cost services outside your category?
- Are substitute offerings improving at a rate that outpaces your ability to raise quality, reduce cost or enhance experience?

- Which customer segments are experimenting with AI-driven alternatives, and what does their early adoption suggest about broader market drift?
- How often are customers choosing simpler, cheaper AI-enabled substitutes for tasks or outcomes you currently monetise?
- If substitutes improved by 10 to 20 per cent, which parts of your proposition would customers stop paying for first?

Metrics that matter

- **Substitutability index:** Percentage of your value chain elements that can already be replicated by AI-powered external alternatives at acceptable quality.
- **Substitute adoption curves:** Rate at which customers are shifting usage, spend or attention to AI-enabled alternatives.
- **Price–value compression ratio:** Extent to which substitutes offer similar or sufficient outcomes at a fraction of the cost, signalling erosion of your pricing power.

Supplier dependence

AI infrastructure is consolidating around a handful of core-model providers. Your cost base, innovation pipeline and even your ethical exposure increasingly depend on supplier decisions over which you have little control. What once was a support function becomes a strategic liability when differentiation sits upstream and bills keep climbing.

Reality-check questions

- Would a pricing increase, API rate-limit change or contract revision from your primary AI supplier create a material cost shock within the next three to six months?

- How many of your core workflows, products or services depend on a single model provider that you could not replace within 60 to 90 days?
- Have vendor roadmap decisions (such as model deprecation, licensing changes or alignment updates) forced you to alter your product strategy or delivery model in the past 12 months?
- How exposed are you to risks of supplier bias, censorship, alignment behaviours or geopolitical shifts baked into the model you rely on?
- What is the volume and sensitivity of organisational data you are placing into external suppliers without full visibility into their data-sovereignty, storage, reuse and exit terms?

Metrics that matter

- **Supplier concentration ratio:** Percentage of your critical capabilities or workflows dependent on one versus multiple model providers.
- **Switching readiness:** Estimated time, cost and business impact of migrating key workflows to an alternative model or internal capability.
- **Upstream cost exposure:** Projected AI cost over the next 12 to 24 months (including supplier pricing, compute, licensing) and its share of your recurring cost base.

Customer expectation delta

One of the most visible pressures to your organisation comes from the growing gap between what your customers now expect and what you can deliver. AI has raised the standard across every interaction. Fast responses, tailored experiences and accurate support feel normal. Customers judge you against the best experience they get anywhere, not just against peers in your sector. When expectations rise faster than your ability to meet them, loyalty dissipates. People do not wait for improvements. They simply move to the option that feels easier and more responsive.

Reality-check questions

- Are customers explicitly comparing your experience to the best digital experiences they have elsewhere, rather than peers in your industry?
- How often do customers request AI-enabled features (summaries, recommendations, faster responses) that you cannot deliver at parity?
- Are frontline teams reporting an increase in customer impatience or intolerance for delays that would have been acceptable 18 months ago?
- Have your improvements in internal performance metrics failed to meaningfully shift customer satisfaction or NPS?
- If a competitor offered an AI-enabled, step-change experience tomorrow, how vulnerable would you be to silent churn?

Metrics that matter

- **Expectation gap:** Difference between customer expectations (measured via surveys and interviews) and current capability.
- **Silent churn rate:** Customers leaving without complaints or feedback.
- **Experience parity:** Comparison of your response time, personalisation, accuracy and proactivity versus AI-enhanced competitors.

Putting it all together: Reading your velocity

The DVI is not a scorecard. It is a sensing tool. The goal is not to label your organisation as safe or unsafe. It is to understand the pattern of acceleration. A high score in one dimension is manageable. A high score in two is uncomfortable. A high score across three or more means your platform is burning faster than your current decision rhythm. Remember also the point of the DVI is to encourage discussion and surface blind spots. If you don't know, for example, what public AI tools are available that would enable a rival team to build a MVP of your offering, this is your signal to find out.

Leaders who use the DVI well do three things:

1. **They track velocity regularly.** Disruption is not an annual assessment. It is a monthly one.
2. **They respond proportionally.** High velocity demands faster decision rights, tighter feedback loops and more frequent strategy dialogues.
3. **They use the DVI to set the agenda, rather than fuel panic.** The aim is clarity and not drama.

The DVI links directly to the chapters that follow. Once you understand your disruption velocity, you can define safe automation boundaries, calibrate your strategic tempo and make deliberate choices about transformation sequencing. In short, you gain the ability to act before the fire reaches the structure, rather than after.

Application: Applying the heat map to your business model

The AI Disruption Velocity Index becomes useful only when it begins to shape decisions. A diagnostic is meaningless unless it changes the way you as a leader allocate attention, sequence initiatives and adjust your organisation's rhythm. The DVI is designed to help you do exactly that. It allows you to translate vague unease into clear signals and replace instinct with evidence. This section shows how to use the heat map effectively, interpret the patterns it reveals, and turn velocity into movement before the organisation starts to strain.

Run the DVI honestly

The DVI works best when you and other leaders in your organisation treat it as a field assessment rather than a performance review. The objective is not to protect a narrative, defend past decisions or justify an existing strategy. It is to see the landscape as it is. That requires realistic scoring and specific examples, rather than wishful thinking. **When you and your team speak plainly about what they observe in the market, the velocity becomes visible.** When you default to optimism, the signals flatten and the map loses value. Honesty is the advantage here. Blind spots are the risk.

Assess each force with evidence

Each of the five forces offers a different window into where pressure is building and how quickly it is moving. You do not need exhaustive datasets or complex modelling. You need a handful of grounded examples that cut through internal narratives and reveal what is actually happening in the market.

The aim is to replace broad generalisations with concrete, observable behaviour so you and your organisation can see the shape of the change rather than debate its existence. When the evidence is specific, the signals become clearer and the conversation becomes more honest.

Competition

What are your competitors really doing? Look past their public statements and pay attention to their behaviour. If they are improving their offer faster than you can match, the basis of competition has already changed. When they increase value while lowering cost, the gap widens. And when customers who once felt loyal begin moving towards them without hesitation, you are already competing on new terms. These signals rarely arrive as bold announcements. They show up in cadence, pricing, product momentum and the ease with which customers drift towards them without fanfare. When competitors begin to accelerate, you usually see it first at the edges and not in the headlines.

New entrants

Look to the edges of your market, because this is where disruption usually appears first. AI now allows very small teams to build credible products with a fraction of the resources once required. The barrier to entry is no longer scale or capital, but simply motivation and access to the right tools. When adjacent players start drifting into your space, when new teams produce high-quality prototypes in weeks or when customers begin assembling their own lightweight alternatives, the signals are clear. The assumptions that once protected your moat are already weakening.

Substitutes

Substitutes rarely arrive as a direct challenge. They emerge quietly through convenience. Customers try an alternative for a single task because it is quicker or cheaper. Then they use it again. Over time, those small experiments accumulate into new habits. Bit by bit, the definition of what counts as 'good enough' shifts. Once customers recalibrate their expectations around these new options, your value proposition weakens even if your product has not changed at all.

Suppliers

Your resilience now depends heavily on decisions made upstream. If a single platform's pricing change, API rate limit or model retirement can alter your economics overnight, the dependency is already deeper than you think. These shifts rarely come with warning. They are implemented globally and instantly, with limited room for negotiation. What feels like a convenient integration today can become a structural constraint tomorrow. Supplier risk is quiet until the moment it is not, and by then your options are usually narrow and expensive.

Customers

Finally, assess expectation drift. Customers no longer judge you only against peers in your sector. They benchmark you against the best digital experiences they encounter anywhere. When that baseline moves, it moves for everyone. Silent churn, stagnating satisfaction despite improvements and rising impatience at the frontline are all early warnings that expectations have shifted beyond your current capability. These signals are subtle at first, but they harden quickly. Once customers have experienced a faster, clearer or more personalised alternative, they do not revert. You cannot negotiate them back to earlier expectations. The standard has already reset.

Look for patterns, not scores

Once the five forces have been assessed, step back and look at how they interact. Disruption velocity is rarely isolated. It clusters. The power of the DVI lies in revealing these clusters before they become unavoidable.

Remember that patterns matter more than individual scores:

- A single elevated force may be noise.
- Two elevated forces indicate a direction of travel.
- Three or more indicate a structural shift.

Remember also that certain combinations carry particular weight:

- Competitive acceleration paired with rising substitutes signals margin pressure.
- A widening expectation delta combined with supplier dependence signals fragility.
- Entrants rising alongside new substitutes signals erosion of the entire business model.

When multiple forces move together, the question is no longer whether to act but how quickly.

Turn the heat map into priorities

The DVI becomes valuable when velocity shapes the agenda. High-velocity forces demand earlier action, clearer trade-offs and more leadership time. This is often where organisations struggle. They acknowledge the heat but continue resourcing the familiar. Don't fall into this trap and, instead, take decisive action:

- If substitutes rise, invest in augmentation and experience layers that differentiate your organisation beyond functional output.
- If competitors accelerate, compress cycle times and remove bottlenecks that slow releases.
- If expectations jump, lift the service baseline before focusing on efficiency.
- If supplier dependence is high, diversify or build minimal internal capability to restore resilience.

The most effective executive teams connect the DVI directly to their AI initiative portfolio. They ensure that work that addresses high-velocity forces moves up the queue. Work in low-velocity areas is paused or simplified. Scarce transformation capacity is pointed towards the parts of the business model under the greatest pressure, and not the parts that shout loudest.

Reset your decision rhythm

No organisation can respond effectively to a fast market with a slow decision cadence. Annual strategy cycles are too long. Multi-year roadmaps are too rigid. A slow rhythm inside a fast landscape creates the conditions for disruption.

A more suitable cadence combines monthly sensing, quarterly strategic recalibration and weekly experiments. Fast cycles do not guarantee success, but they do create the conditions for learning, which is what disruption now demands.

Keep the DVI alive

The DVI is not an annual workshop. It is a monthly discipline. Someone must own it, update it and surface new patterns early. A living heat map reduces drift and creates organisational immunity. You and your organisation can then match your decisions to the rhythm of the environment, rather than the comfort of the calendar.

The DVI does not eliminate uncertainty. It removes ambiguity. It ensures you as a leader can see pressure forming before it becomes damage and gives you and your organisation enough time to adjust.

Playbook: Reading the heat before it burns you

Here's how to use the DVI as a heat map to set priorities in your organisation:

1. **Run the DVI every month, not every year:** Treat disruption velocity as a leading indicator. Schedule a short, disciplined monthly review with the same group of senior leaders. This seems excessive – it isn't. Keep the scoring consistent. Keep the conversation grounded in evidence. The aim is continuity rather than ceremony.
2. **Isolate the two forces moving fastest:** Do not try to fix everything at once. Identify the two highest velocity forces and focus your response there. Competitive acceleration and substitute speed usually signal

immediate margin risk. Customer expectation gaps and supplier dependence often signal experience and resilience risk.

3. **Match your tempo to the velocity:** Increase the rhythm of decision-making when the heat map spikes. Move from annual cycles to quarterly resets. Shift from large programs to short experiments. Tighten feedback loops so learning compounds rather than stalls.
4. **Reallocate resources towards high-heat zones:** Direct budget, talent and executive attention to the areas where velocity is highest. If customers have already reset expectations, prioritise experience uplift. If substitutes are rising, invest in augmentation and differentiation layers before efficiency plays.
5. **Make the DVI a leadership habit:** Assign a single-owner DVI process. Maintain a live heat map. Use it to set agendas, not decorate slides. When disruption velocity becomes routine executive practice, you move before the fire spreads rather than after it burns.

Provocation: Your platform is already burning

The uncomfortable truth is that disruption does not arrive with a press release. It gathers quietly, in the gaps between meetings, in the delays between decisions and in the excuses leaders tell themselves about why the pace of change will slow. By the time the signals reach the board papers, the real damage has already been done. **AI has shifted the burden of proof. You no longer need evidence to act. You need evidence to wait.**

This is the moment to decide what kind of leader you intend to be. You can treat AI as noise, something to monitor while you protect the status quo. Or you can treat it as the new operating context, something that demands a different rhythm, a different level of curiosity and a different relationship with risk. The leaders who wait for certainty are already behind. The leaders who move early are not being reckless. They are recognising that indecision is now the riskiest posture of all.

The provocation is simple: assume your platform is already burning. Assume competition has changed. Assume expectations have moved. Assume substitutes are rising faster than your internal capability. These assumptions are not pessimistic. They are your new baseline for strategic judgement. When you start from this position, your decisions become sharper. Your tempo increases. Your organisation becomes harder to catch off guard.

Remember:

- **You do not need a perfect AI strategy.** You need a learning system.
- **You do not need a five-year roadmap.** You need a 90-day cycle.
- **You do not need to predict the future.** You need to respond to the present.

If you are still debating whether your platform is burning, the answer is yes. The only real question is whether you move while the heat is manageable or wait until the structure gives way.

What's next

Understanding disruption velocity tells you how quickly pressure is building. But speed alone does not tell you where to aim. Moving faster without direction only compounds noise. The next chapter shifts the focus from heat to intent. It argues that AI advantage does not start with tools, platforms or pilots, but with a clear view of what you are trying to make possible over the next 12 months. Before you accelerate, you need separation between strategy and technology, a deliberate North Star and a portfolio that turns capability into momentum. The question now is not how advanced your AI is, but whether it is pointed anywhere that matters.

CHAPTER 5

Strategy before tools

I love buying gadgets. Whenever I take up a new hobby, I go straight to the gear. Whether that new hobby is scuba diving, rock climbing, music or cooking, it doesn't matter. If a potential piece of equipment comes with a review section, I will find it. If a forum thread is arguing about the best version, I will read it. If a YouTube channel is dedicated to unboxing that equipment, I will somehow watch all of it.

Choosing the gear feels like momentum. It is tangible. It is measurable. It arrives in a box. You can point at it and say, progress.

Recently, for example, I decided to learn to play the piano. So I did what any sensible adult does. I spent days researching what kind of piano I should buy. I watched far too much YouTube. I went into music stores and asked questions. I compared action, sound engines and pedal response like I had a performance at the Sydney Opera House next week.

Then I finally bought one. The only issue was that I had not really thought too much about what music I wanted to play, or how I was even going to learn. I hadn't decided on a genre or even a song. I didn't even have a vague intention like, 'I want to be able to play for friends without causing them to leave the room'. I had optimised the instrument before deciding the outcome, and had become extremely well informed about a problem I did not yet have.

I see the same thing in my consulting work. Many clients naturally see AI as a technology – and it is hard not to. Of course it is a technological marvel. It is also new enough to trigger that same 'new gear' instinct. The questions come quickly and predictably. What tools do you use? Do you prefer ChatGPT or Claude? What do you think about Microsoft Copilot? Should we build on one platform or hedge across several? What models are the best this month? Which vendor will win?

While these are interesting questions, they are not the main event.

AI technology matters, but it is rarely the constraint. Most organisations do not fail with AI because they chose the wrong tool. They fail because they didn't choose the right destination. They delegated the work to the CTO, which is a reasonable instinct, and then stayed comfortably upstream of the harder discussion – the kind that asks what they actually want AI to make possible. Where do we need to be in the next 12 months? What advantage are we trying to create? What are we willing to stop so that the important work can progress?

Tools are easier than intent. Gear is easier than practice. A new piano is much easier than learning to play. That is the trap AI sets. It offers endless capability and a constant stream of shiny choices. It invites you to optimise the instrument while avoiding the question of the music.

The leaders who get this right start in a different place. They begin with a short, deliberate ambition – a North Star close enough to reach. Then they choose the tools, the bets and the rhythm that can actually get them there.

Restoring separation before you accelerate

The conversation about AI and strategy inside senior teams carries a particular tension; not urgency or confidence but something more hesitant. Leaders agree it matters, yet the significance keeps slipping out of view. One moment the discussion narrows to models, data and tooling. Next, it widens to competition and pace. The two threads wrap around each other and the clarity needed for real decisions evaporates.

The result is a pattern that can be seen everywhere. Some organisations move quickly, collecting pilots like souvenirs. Each one is proof of effort, neatly packaged for a board paper, yet none of them add up to a strategy. Others move slowly, worried that a premature decision will lock them into the wrong architecture or expose them to unnecessary risk. They pause and then pause again, waiting for certainty that never arrives.

Both reactions stem from the same misunderstanding. AI is treated as if it were a single problem or a single opportunity. It becomes a domain to be delegated to the technologists. In reality, it shows up in two forms: it is a technical capability that demands careful design, and it is a strategic catalyst that reshapes where you play and how you win.

When these two faces collapse into one conversation, progress stalls. Technical debates drown out strategic intent. Strategy drifts away from capability. Decisions slow and alignment frays. AI becomes a haze of ambition and anxiety rather than a lever for clarity.

The path forward starts with restoring that separation. Recognising the distinction allows you as a leader to see where speed helps, where restraint protects and where noise can be ignored. It sharpens your choices about what to automate, what to amplify and what to safeguard. It turns motion into movement and activity into advantage.

Two faces, one problem

AI, it turns out, is a double act. On one side it is technical, providing systems, infrastructure, models and the plumbing that keeps them alive. It sits naturally with the CTO because it behaves as technology always has. It needs architecture, governance, data quality and the steady discipline of engineering. That face is familiar. It gives you tools. It shapes what is possible inside the organisation. It creates capability.

On the other hand, AI is also a strategy catalyst. It reshapes the questions of where to play, how to differentiate and which parts of the business should be protected, automated or reinvented. It changes the economics of markets, the expectations of customers and the tempo at which competitors can move. This face is less familiar. It doesn't require a technical decision but is instead a question of intent. It forces you to think about purpose, advantage and direction for your organisation.

Both faces of AI matter. Both are essential. Yet when leaders treat them as one, things become confused. Technical debates swamp strategic conversations. Strategic ambition outpaces delivery. Decisions slow because no-one is quite sure whether they are discussing architecture or advantage. The organisation drifts into a holding pattern, not because it lacks intelligence but because the categories themselves have blurred. When the line between tools and direction disappears, momentum follows it out the door.

So the real question is not what AI can do. That list grows longer by the week and is of limited strategic value. The more important question is what your organisation wants AI to make possible. That framing pulls attention back to outcomes rather than features. It sharpens the need for a North Star that actually guides investment decisions. It makes the inspection of moats more disciplined. It forces a portfolio approach that balances optimisation, acceleration and transformation rather than defaulting to whichever projects happen to be loudest.

The aim is not activity. It is strategic velocity. The organisations that benefit most from AI are not the ones that do the most, but the ones that move with purpose.

Why now: The illusion of progress

Most organisations are not short of AI activity. They are short of intent. The tooling conversation is loud, visible and strangely comforting. It produces pilots, proofs and platform decisions that look like momentum. Yet without a clear view of where you need to be in the next 12 months, that motion rarely turns into advantage.

Business planning used to move predictably. Strategy cycles stretched for years and annual plans felt like comfortable anchors. Now, those plans burn out in months. The digital roadmap that once seemed visionary is out of date before you can implement it. By the time the board sees the slides, the world outside has already moved on.

That shift is not theoretical. It shows up in the widening gap between how fast markets move and how slowly organisations adjust. The signals arrive sooner. Customer behaviour changes earlier. Competitors experiment more aggressively. Yet the internal machinery of planning still assumes you have time to debate, align and refine before committing. That assumption does more than slow you down. It allows activity to substitute for direction.

AI isn't conjuring up new forces; it's pressing fast-forward on the ones already at play. Competitors use it to shrink timelines, customers use it to raise the bar and markets now punish hesitation. At the same time, the abundance of tools makes it easy to confuse capability with strategy.

Speed becomes a multiplier. A small improvement compounds through hundreds of processes. A single automation frees capacity that can be reinvested. A modest product enhancement shifts customer expectations across an entire category. These changes used to take years. AI compresses them into a quarter. Even a slight lag in response becomes a meaningful disadvantage because rivals are not only moving faster but also learning faster. If you have not defined what you are trying to make possible over the next 12 months, you cannot tell whether you are learning or just experimenting.

The gap is widening not between the bold and the cautious, but between those who adapt and those who analyse. Every quarter spent in debate is a quarter your rivals spend learning. Every experiment you delay is a lesson they learn and you don't. And every pilot you run without a North Star becomes another neatly packaged artefact with no compounding value.

This is the new asymmetry. Fast learners build confidence through evidence. Slow movers build anxiety through conjecture. The longer the delay, the more your organisation defaults to risk avoidance, which slows it further. By the time a decision is finally made, the opportunity has often shifted, shrunk or vanished. The drift is rarely dramatic. It is simply persistent.

Here's the uncomfortable truth: advantage doesn't erode anymore; it evaporates. Margins, business models and even reputations now have half-lives measured in quarters, not years. Evaporation does not require a better model on the other side. It only requires you to be directionless for long enough.

Yet most strategy still moves at a human pace built for careful deliberation, rather than rapid iteration. Alignment is prized over acceleration. That made sense when information was scarce and the world moved predictably. But in a landscape where intelligence compounds and technology learns faster than we do, the old tempo just can't keep up. You cannot govern AI if you cannot articulate a 12-month intent.

The biggest shift AI brings isn't new competition; it's a new tempo. The real question isn't whether your strategy will need to change, but whether your organisation can change quickly enough to keep it alive. That change starts upstream, with intent, rather than downstream, with tools.

That is why AI can't stay locked in the server room. It belongs at the centre of the board and executive conversation. The challenge now isn't just adopting new tools, but also designing a new rhythm. A rhythm anchored in outcomes, not features.

The framework: The AI transformation blueprint

If AI is changing the tempo of competition, you need a way to keep up as a leader. That starts with three disciplines: setting direction, protecting differentiation and rebalancing effort.

These disciplines are not theoretical. They are practical actions that allow your organisation to move at a tempo that matches the market without sacrificing judgement or drifting into chaos. They give you a way to make decisions at speed without turning strategy into improvisation. They translate the abstractions of AI into choices that can be acted on in weeks, not years. In a landscape where learning cycles are short, these disciplines become the scaffolding for clarity, and provide the AI transformation blueprint shown in the figure opposite.

Set your North Star

Before you automate anything, define your direction. Your 'North Star' should be a 12- to 18-month aspiration. Where you and your organisation are headed should be bold enough to inspire and close enough to execute. Forget three- to five-year plans.

The AI transformation blueprint – connecting ambition to execution

Drivers and threats: What will and won't change?

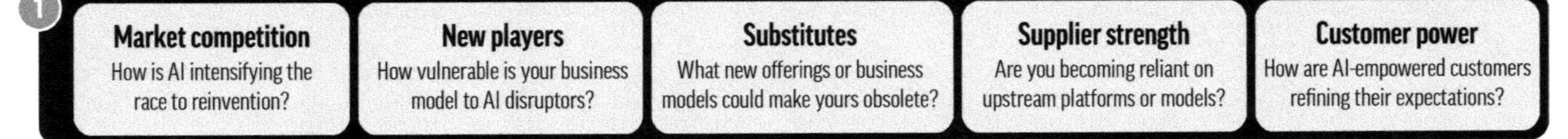

Game plan: Where are you heading and why will you win?

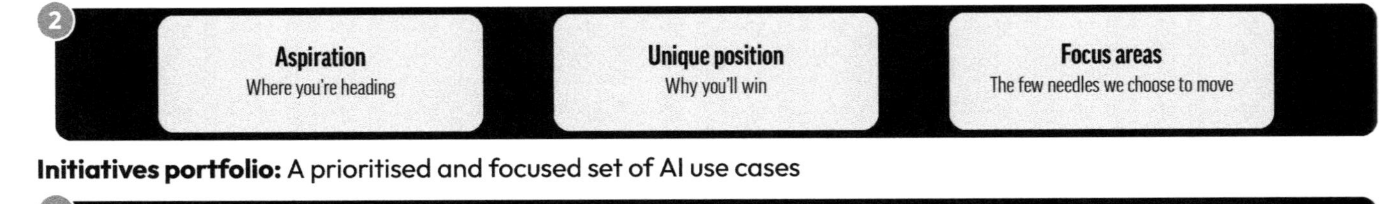

Initiatives portfolio: A prioritised and focused set of AI use cases

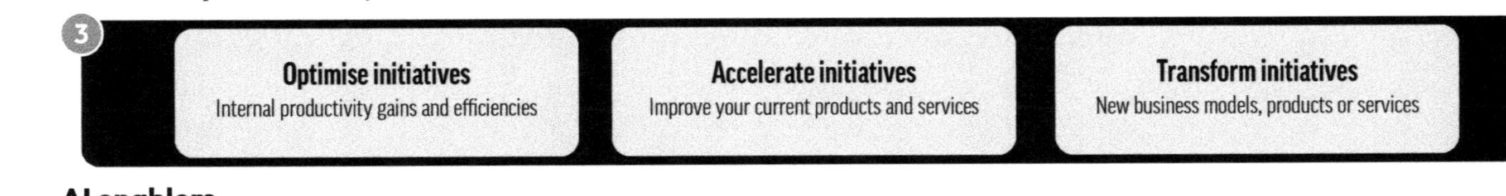

AI enablers

Most strategic failures begin with an unclear destination. This happens not because the organisation lacks ambition, but because ambition floats freely without shape or boundary. AI amplifies this weakness. It gives everyone something shiny and new to chase. It fills backlogs with ideas that feel promising but do not add up to anything tangible. Defining your North Star counters that drift by concentrating attention on what actually matters.

A strong North Star is:

- specific enough to focus resources
- ambitious enough to energise people
- testable enough to measure progress.

Each of these criterion plays a different role. Specificity narrows the field of choice so that teams can commit rather than hedge. Ambition lifts your organisation out of incrementalism and provides the emotional energy needed to sustain effort. Testability prevents the North Star from becoming a slogan, and instead forces evidence, inspection and accountability.

Think of your North Star as a living hypothesis, not a monument. Without this anchor, every AI project is just wasted activity without direction.

A North Star also creates an honest filter, revealing which opportunities genuinely align to the future the organisation is trying to create and which are distractions dressed up as innovation. Without such a filter, everything looks attractive, which is the fastest route to dilution. AI produces a steady stream of possibilities. The North Star helps determine which ones deserve attention.

Direction creates discipline. It is the simplest starting point and the most neglected.

Re-evaluate your moats to protect differentiation

Every company likes to believe it has a moat of differentiation. But AI is quietly lowering the water, exposing which defences still hold and which were delusional.

This exposure does not happen all at once. It unfolds through small signals. Customers begin switching more easily. Competitors release products faster than expected. Sales cycles shorten in ways that suggest alternatives are becoming more attractive. These early signals often arrive long before the numbers change. Organisations that ignore them underestimate their resilience.

The classic sources of advantage are being reshaped by AI, automation, data and speed in the following ways:

- **Cost advantage:** Being low-cost is no longer enough. AI makes cost reduction easier to replicate. The advantage is how fast you convert savings into new value. Savings that sit still shrink. Savings that are reinvested create lift.
- **Switching costs:** Integrations, APIs and interoperability are eroding lock-in and reducing switching costs. Customer loyalty now depends less on friction and more on the continuous delivery of value. Switching costs have not disappeared, but they no longer operate as a barrier. They operate as an inconvenience. AI-enabled challengers treat inconvenience as an invitation.
- **Network effects:** Networks still matter but the flywheel runs on learning rate, not just user count. The biggest network

is not automatically the best network. If a competitor learns faster per interaction, your scale becomes less protective.

- **Intangible assets and brand:** Trust and authenticity are the new scarce resources. In a world full of AI slop, customers cling to signals of empathy and credibility. Do not underestimate this. The organisations that protect trust with discipline will gain an advantage that AI cannot imitate.
- **Efficient scale:** Automation lets smaller players operate at enterprise scale. Scale remains an advantage only if it fuels adaptability and not inertia. Size without speed becomes sentimental.

As a leader, ask yourself:

- Which of our moats are strengthening, and which are dissolving as a result of AI?
- What data advantages can we build that compound over time?
- What kind of trust will our customers still value when AI can do mostly everything else?

A sober re-evaluation is not an exercise in pessimism. It is a diagnostic. It clarifies where advantage genuinely sits and identifies the foundations that can support new growth. It also exposes the assumptions that have quietly expired. Many organisations discover that due to AI their moats are shallower than they thought. That discovery is not a failure. It is the moment where real strategy begins.

Once you understand the truth of your position, you can choose which advantages to reinforce, which to abandon and which to redesign.

Focus your portfolio to match reality

Once your North Star and competitive differentiators are clear, shape your portfolio. The goal is not perfect balance but deliberate coverage. Without it, organisations drift towards one extreme or the other. They either bury themselves in efficiency projects or leap prematurely into reinvention without the capability to sustain it. Both paths look productive. Both create risk. Coverage across the three horizons is what converts activity into advantage.

Every organisation should have AI initiatives in each of the following three categories:

1. **Optimise initiatives:** These should be focused on productivity and operational efficiency. Automate workflows, streamline reporting and reduce repetitive analysis. These initiatives free capacity and create headroom for reinvestment. They are essential in low-disruption environments where efficiency is still an advantage. They also create the financial and operational runway needed for bigger bets. Optimisation is the quiet engine room of AI strategy.
2. **Accelerate initiatives:** These enhance the customer value proposition. Add AI to existing products and services to create smarter, more personalised and faster experiences. This is where your organisation can begin to compete on intelligence rather than scale. Acceleration builds relevance. It keeps your organisation in the consideration set and signals progress without forcing a full reinvention.
3. **Transform initiatives:** These are focused on reinventing the business or operating model itself. Use AI to create entirely new products, pricing models or ways of working. Enter

markets that were once too costly to access. Transformation initiatives demand courage and strong governance. They are how incumbents build future moats before others do. They ask you to imagine the business not as it is, but as it could be if the constraints changed.

You will need to determine the mix of initiatives your organisation adopts. No universal formula exists and the right mix depends on your context and on how much your industry and, specifically, your business model is being disrupted by AI. However, here's a rough guide, based on level of disruption:

- **Low disruption:** Weight your portfolio towards optimise and accelerate initiatives to strengthen your organisational core.
- **Moderate disruption:** Maintain meaningful coverage across all three, with enough weight on transform to preserve optionality.
- **High disruption:** Weight your portfolio towards transform initiatives to reinvent your business model before others redefine the market.

The portfolio mix of initiatives tells a story about what you value and where you're headed.

Lean too far into optimisation and you're just managing decline. My belief is that AI-driven productivity is simply a ticket to play and will ultimately be competitively neutral. Lean too far into transformation and you risk losing trust. Strategy at machine speed is about holding the tension, and ensuring near-term gains fund longer-term advantage.

The AI initiative portfolio becomes the heartbeat of your organisation. It keeps the strategy grounded and forces you and other leaders to make choices. It pushes funding towards initiatives that create real momentum. It allocates talent to the places where learning matters most. It gives teams clarity on why certain projects move forward and others do not. Above all, it ensures that speed has purpose instead of panic.

Application: Turning direction into momentum

Clarity, on its own, is just a nice idea. The real challenge is turning ambition into action.

Most organisations stop at clarity. They agree on a direction, write an impressive document and present a series of initiatives that appear aligned. Then everything slows. Momentum disperses across functions. Urgency dissolves across competing priorities. The gap between the strategic intent and the operating reality widens in silence. AI exposes this gap faster than anything that came before it. The organisations that thrive are the ones that get shit done.

Turning strategy into action rests on four operating muscles: time, connection, learning and leadership.

Reset the strategy cycle

Taking action starts with time. The three-year strategy cycle is over. The fastest learners work in rolling 90-day sprints, always testing, always adjusting. For them, strategy isn't a document but a behaviour, lived out week by week.

This does not mean abandoning long-term planning. It means complementing it with shorter loops that keep the organisation aligned to reality. A 90-day cycle forces decisions to move. It limits the temptation to wait for perfect information. It pushes you to make smaller bets more often, and it keeps your team focused on progress rather than polish.

A shorter cycle also exposes drift early. It shows which initiatives are stalled, which teams need support and which assumptions no longer hold. This level of visibility reduces political risk. It becomes easier to adjust, not because you and your team are more bold, but because the cadence makes adjustment normal.

Create a direct line to the North Star

Next is connection. You should be able to draw a clear line from every AI initiative back to your organisation's North Star, not just to a department's wish list. If you can't, it's just noise.

This line of sight is where focus comes from. Without it, teams default to what is interesting rather than what is essential. AI makes this temptation sharper because the opportunities multiply quickly. Connection keeps effort coherent. It stops teams from chasing every model update or vendor promise and instead anchors decisions in purpose.

As leader, you should ask three simple questions of every initiative:

1. What part of the North Star does this advance?
2. How will we know it is working?
3. What are we willing to stop to make room for it?

Most organisations can answer the first question. Few answer the third. The discipline of stopping is what turns strategy into movement. Without it, the portfolio bloats and momentum stalls.

Shift from activity to discovery

After time and connection comes learning. The most forward-thinking organisations don't count activity; they count discovery. Their leaders ask, 'What did we learn this week that changes what we'll do next?' This shift from planning to proving may be subtle, but it is a radical one.

Discovery reframes performance. It rewards evidence over optimism. It pushes teams to test the parts of their work that feel most fragile, and encourages them to expose risks early rather than hide them. AI accelerates learning when it is used deliberately. It also accelerates waste when it is used without direction.

A discovery mindset shrinks the cost of being wrong. It encourages small experiments and reduces the fear that slows decisions. It makes change normal rather than exceptional. Over time, this mindset builds organisational confidence because teams see that adjustment is not failure but how progress is made.

Lead for speed, not pressure

The final element is leadership. AI strategy isn't about pushing people harder; it's about clearing the path. The best leaders remove friction, align incentives and give teams the freedom to move faster than the old rules would ever allow.

Leadership at this tempo looks different. It is less about sponsorship and visibility, and more about simplification and decision rights. It is less about owning the plan and more about owning the environment in which the plan moves.

Your old reflex may have been to create more oversight. Your new reflex now needs to be to reduce unnecessary steps. The old model rewarded caution. The new model rewards clarity. You set the tempo through the constraints you remove, not the urgency you broadcast.

Converting rhythm into results

In the end, speed is just discipline in a new form. The discipline shows up in weekly operating rhythms where teams review learning, not slides. It shows up in monthly checkpoints where the portfolio is adjusted, not defended. It shows up in quarterly decisions where resources shift to match evidence, not politics. These rituals keep strategy alive. They stop it from becoming a static document and turn it into a continuous conversation anchored in action.

Momentum comes from the combination of pace and purpose. One without the other creates churn. Together, they create advantage. AI makes the need for that advantage sharper because the organisations that move first gather more information, refine their assumptions and widen the gap.

Strategy at machine speed is not about being reckless. It is about being responsive. It is about replacing delay with discovery and replacing certainty with evidence. It turns direction into momentum by making progress inevitable rather than optional.

Playbook: The moves that keep you ahead

Treat this as the bare minimum required to keep your strategy alive in an AI-shaped market:

1. **Define the North Star:** Create a clear 12- to 18-month aspiration tied to measurable outcomes. This becomes your North Star, and should be specific enough to focus investment and simple enough to energise teams. A North Star that cannot be tested becomes decoration. One that drives choices becomes momentum.
2. **Re-examine your moats:** Identify your true differentiation, and what is eroding and what is emerging. Inspect how data, learning speed and trust shape your position. The moats that survive AI are the ones that compound. Everything else is sentiment.
3. **Shape the portfolio:** Ensure you have initiatives across optimise, accelerate and transform. The mix should reflect the disruption reality your sector or company faces. Coverage prevents you defaulting to productivity theatre or premature reinvention, and keeps effort anchored to both near-term outcomes and longer-term advantage.
4. **Kill the zombies:** End legacy projects that drain focus or talent. These are the initiatives that no longer align to the North Star but survive through habit. Clearing them creates space for work that matters.
5. **Measure learning velocity:** Track the time from idea to insight as your core KPI. Activity is not progress.

Discovery is. The organisations that learn faster decide faster.

Provocation: Act before you're ready

AI isn't coming for your job. It is coming for your indecision. It rewards those who choose a direction, and it punishes those who hide behind activity.

That shift is uncomfortable because most organisations were built on a different philosophy. They were designed to minimise error rather than maximise learning. They were shaped by governance models that prized alignment over adaptation. In that world, waiting looked sensible. In this one, waiting is the most costly option. Delay creates gaps that widen quietly at first, and then suddenly. By the time you feel the impact, the compounding has already happened elsewhere.

The organisations that thrive will not be the ones with the most AI. They will be the ones with the clearest intent. They will use AI as a strategy catalyst, not a technology hobby. They will set a near-term ambition that can be executed, and then build a portfolio of bets that serves it. Some will optimise. Some will accelerate. Some will transform. The mix will reflect their reality, not their enthusiasm.

For them, strategy becomes a living experiment. A sequence of bets, each one designed to uncover what works next. They operate on the assumption that the first idea is rarely the right one. They assume that value emerges through iteration, not prediction. They do not wait for alignment to be perfect before acting. They act, and then align around the evidence.

Agility is disciplined intent. It is having a North Star close enough to reach and the courage to adjust as new evidence appears. It is the willingness to treat certainty as a luxury rather than a prerequisite. It is the acceptance that progress is uneven, sometimes untidy, but always directional.

The leaders who win will not be the loudest futurists or the deepest technologists. They will be the ones who separate tools from direction, and use evidence to keep the strategy alive.

In the end, AI does not reward the most intelligent organisations. It rewards those who act with intelligence.

What's next

Direction is only meaningful once it meets real work, real people and real consequences. Once you have intent, how do you apply AI inside the organisation without creating confident mistakes at scale? The next chapter moves from North Stars to the shop floor. It shows why the same tool produces wildly different outcomes depending on whose hands it lands in, and why careless rollout quietly destroys judgement even as output rises. It then offers a disciplined starting point: decide what to automate, who to augment and what must stay human because trust depends on it, and begin where the problem already has the budget so proof funds your ambition.

Scalpels need surgeons

In my adult life, I have owned a few houses – and this is where the problems start. I am not a handyman. I am the sort of person who can turn a simple home repair job into a cautionary tale. My best work usually ends with a call to a qualified tradesperson to clean up my mess. My worst work ends with a trip to hospital. I will not say which is more common. My dignity prefers uncertainty.

My shed at home is littered with power tools – electric drills, power saws, even an angle grinder. I do not know why I own an angle grinder. I have never looked at a household task and thought, *You know what this needs? Sparks.* Yet there it is, sitting on the shelf like a small, angry promise.

The tools give me a false sense of competence. Put a drop saw in my hands and I can look like I know what I am doing. For a brief moment, I even believe it. I have my safety glasses on, measuring tape clipped to my belt, and I feel like I belong on a building site. Then reality arrives. The cut is wrong. The timber splinters. The line I swore was straight begins to drift like a bad decision made at Bunnings.

Now put those same tools in the hands of a qualified carpenter and the outcome is almost unfair. Skirting boards appear as if they were always there. Decks line up perfectly. Bathrooms get rebuilt without drama. When a tradie upgrades their tools, their productivity rises and their craft sharpens. They become more precise, faster and cleaner. The tool is an amplifier of skill.

When I upgrade my tools, I simply increase the speed at which I can create problems.

That is the parallel most organisations miss when they rush into AI. The tool is not the strategy. It is not even the capability. It is an amplifier. In the wrong hands, it creates confident mistakes at scale. However, in the right hands, it creates leverage. The difference is not the model but the judgement behind it.

Give AI to a junior team member with limited real-world experience and you can get an artificial bump in output. They may sound sharper, move faster and produce more, but speed is not the same as competence. The risk is not just that they miss an AI hallucination or accept a confident answer they do not understand. The deeper risk is quieter. They stop building judgement. They stop developing instinct. They become operators of automation rather than builders of experience – in other words, they become lemmings. Over time, the organisation gains efficiency and loses depth. That trade rarely shows up on a dashboard until it is too late.

Now give the same AI capability to an experienced professional and something else happens. Their output explodes and creativity lifts. Their decision quality improves because they know what to ask, what to ignore and what to challenge. They can sense when an answer is plausible but wrong. They can bring context that the machine does not have. They do not outsource responsibility. They use the tool to extend their reach.

Same tool, different result.

In earlier chapters, I outlined how AI is shifting work away from expertise and towards judgement, decision quality and relationships. This chapter brings that argument down to ground level. It answers the question every executive eventually asks, usually after the third pilot and the fifth steering committee: how do we actually apply AI inside the organisation without creating chaos?

The answer is not a longer list of use cases. It is a clearer view of work. It is knowing what can be automated and augmented, and what must stay human because trust depends on it. It is starting where the problem already has a budget, so momentum funds itself and belief grows naturally. And it is making sure the tools end up in the right hands, before someone like me picks up the angle grinder.

Why now: When 'spray and pray' fails

Not long ago, a large professional services firm found itself in the news for all the wrong reasons. They had been paid a serious fee, the sort that buys you a lot of confidence, to produce a report for a client. The report was published online. Then the internet did what the internet does.

People started reading the report, and it soon became clear it contained errors that were not subtle. Even saying it 'contained errors' is generous. Some points were simply made up. The report included the kind of thing an AI model can do when it is trying to be helpful and ends up being creative instead. A few elements in the report felt less like analysis and more like a 'choose your own adventure'.

The funniest part, if you enjoy pain, was that none of this was an AI problem. The model did what models do. It generated plausible text at speed. The human failure came afterwards. Someone junior had used the tool without the experience to spot what was off. Then someone senior signed it off without checking properly. It was a rookie error, and it was inexcusable.

I have worked in firms where similar errors have been made. I even used to be a partner at one, which is why I can say this with affection and accuracy. The problem is never the tool. The problem comes with believing the tool has replaced judgement.

The predictable response to a public embarrassment like this is to ban AI. Leaders reach for the corporate equivalent of putting the drop saw in a locked cabinet. It feels decisive and looks responsible. It also misses the point completely. If your people can publish unverified output, the risk does not live in the model. It lives in your workflow, your decision rights and your supervision discipline.

AI is dangerous when it is given mindlessly to the wrong people and then waved through by the right people who are too busy to look. The answer is not prohibition but deliberate application. It is knowing where automation is safe, where augmentation is powerful, and where human empathy and judgement must stay at the centre because trust depends on it.

This connects directly to return on investment (ROI). In many organisations, AI adoption has become a 'spray and pray' approach. Give it to everyone, let a thousand copilots bloom and then wait for magic to happen. What usually happens instead is noise. Teams work faster, but not better. Output increases, but error rates rise. Leaders spend more time sorting out edge cases and exceptions than they saved in the first place – or, worse, they become paralysed and don't know where to deploy next.

That is how ROI dies: with a slow accumulation of rework and failed pilots.

And when ROI dies, belief dies with it. Leaders start questioning whether AI is worth the trouble. Teams conclude it is just another tool that creates more work. Risk teams clamp down. The organisation retreats into caution, not because AI cannot help but because the first wave was undisciplined.

Deliberate deployment breaks that cycle. **Apply AI where the business is already paying for pain. Put it in the hands of people who can calibrate it. Build the checks that match the consequence.** When leaders choose what to automate, who to augment and what to protect, the returns arrive faster and the risks fall. Proof funds ambition and trust stays intact.

The framework: The intelligent work model

AI is reshaping how work creates value. While it rarely replaces jobs outright, it does change the mix of human and machine effort within them. It alters the centre of gravity, tilting some tasks towards automation, lifting others through augmentation and leaving a core that still depends on human empathy and judgement. The real challenge for you as a leader is knowing when AI should drive and when it should ride along.

The temptation is to automate everything. The discipline is to automate only where the work can bear it.

That is where the Intelligent Work Model, shown in the following figure, comes in. It helps you decide what to automate, what to augment and where only human empathy can make the difference. It does not judge work. It classifies it. It shows you which tasks thrive on machine precision, which depend on human oversight and which rely on human connection. It is not a map of replacement. It is a map of value.

Automation is about letting AI handle high-expertise, rule-based work. This is the work that thrives on precision, consistency and scale. It includes calculations, validations, reconciliations and structured analysis. It frees up time, cost and attention. It also reduces error. But, as discussed in chapter 3, it narrows learning if used without care. When automation takes over too much too soon, the formative work that once built experience disappears. Teams gain speed but lose depth. Leaders need to understand this tension because efficiency without experience becomes fragile.

Augmentation is about giving experienced professionals AI tools so they can think, decide and create at a higher level. It does not remove expertise. It amplifies it. Augmentation works because experts know how to calibrate AI. They know when to trust the output and when to override it. They bring the judgement that AI lacks. Well-designed augmentation lifts the ceiling on human contribution, turning experience into leverage.

Some work will always depend on human connection. Roles built on empathy, negotiation and care rely on relational intelligence, which is the one thing machines cannot copy. People trust people who listen, interpret and support. They trust people who understand nuance, risk and consequence. Empathy is not a soft skill in these contexts. It is a structural moat. These are the places for your most emotionally capable people, with AI supporting at the edges. It enhances, but it never replaces.

As shown in the following figure, the Intelligent Work Model visualises the relationship between expertise, experience and empathy using two axes: human judgement on the *x*-axis and task expertise on the *y*-axis.

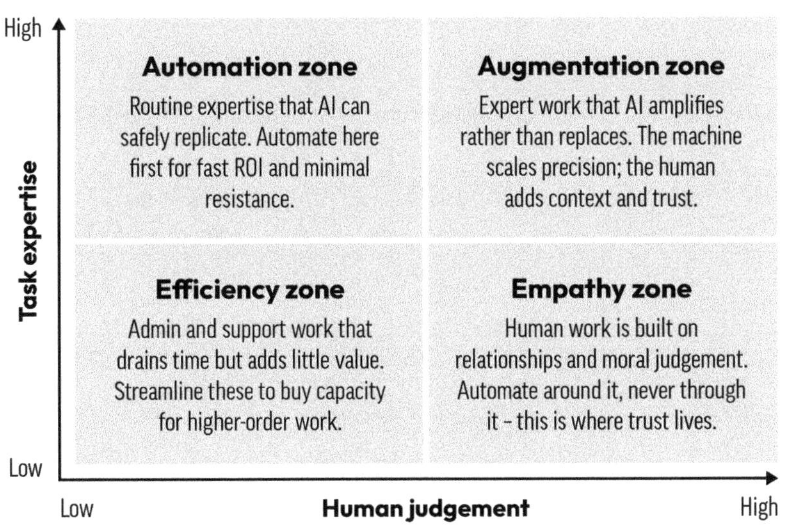

Each quadrant shows a different mode of work and a different role for AI, as follows:

- **Automation zone (high expertise, low experience):** This is the routine expertise that AI can safely replicate. These tasks are well defined. They follow rules and depend on precision rather than judgement. They produce clear outcomes with minimal ambiguity. Automate here first. Doing so delivers fast ROI and minimal resistance. People welcome help with this kind of work because it lowers load without lowering identity. Automation in this zone should create capacity, not controversy.

- **Augmentation zone (high expertise, high experience):** This is the expert work that AI amplifies rather than replaces. These tasks blend deep knowledge with contextual judgement. The tools provide speed, scale and precision. The human adds interpretation, nuance and trust. This is where AI extends human capability rather than supplanting it. Augmentation of tasks in this zone protects experience while increasing its reach. It shortens cycles. It improves decision quality. It lifts the strategic value of experts by shifting their time to what only they can do.
- **Efficiency zone (low expertise, low experience):** This is the admin and support work that drains time but adds little value. These tasks are repetitive and predictable. They are important because they support operations, but they are rarely differentiating. Streamline and eliminate these to free capacity for higher-order work. AI lightens the administrative burden so teams can focus on contribution rather than coordination. The gains here are mostly operational. They build confidence by showing visible improvement quickly.
- **Empathy zone (low expertise, high experience):** This is the quadrant where human judgement and emotional intelligence define the work. These tasks include coaching, negotiation, leadership, care and conflict resolution. The work here carries relational weight, influences trust and affects culture. It shapes decisions that carry consequence. Automate around this zone, not through it. AI can assist with preparation, documentation and insight, but the human must remain at the centre because this is where trust lives.

Think of the model as a compass, not a finish line. It does not tell you what must happen. It tells you what can happen safely. Where expertise dominates, automation brings speed, consistency and scale. It reduces friction and frees resources. Where experience matters most, augmentation turns judgement into leverage, giving experts more scope and sharper tools. And where emotion is at the centre, empathy becomes the moat that protects trust and stability.

Used well, the Intelligent Work Model aligns technology investment with human value. It prevents the familiar mistakes that appear in early AI adoption. It stops you from automating the wrong work and protects your organisation from stripping out the experience they will need later. It frees teams from tasks that AI can handle with ease. Importantly, it keeps the triad of expertise, experience and empathy intact, so capability grows rather than diminishes.

From clarity to conversation

One of the model's greatest strengths is the way it surfaces what must happen first. Most organisations believe they need a long catalogue of use cases. They do not. They need a clear view of where work sits. Once tasks and work are plotted across the four zones, priorities emerge. Automation opportunities become obvious. Augmentation needs stand out. Areas defined by empathy remain visible and protected. Leaders stop guessing and start allocating effort in line with value.

This clarity also reshapes the conversations leadership teams have about AI. Instead of debating tools, they discuss outcomes. Instead of defending familiar ways of working, they examine what the work actually requires. Arguments about risk shift from speculation to assessment of the experience footprint. The tone moves from apprehension to focus. People begin looking at work through its real demands rather than through personal preference or habit.

Protecting capability and guiding pace

The Intelligent Work Model also exposes the early signs of experience scarcity. As emphasised through this book, when automation strips away the centre of work, junior staff lose the tasks that once built their judgement. Without deliberate augmentation, they risk becoming operators of automation rather than builders of experience. By highlighting these gaps early, you can preserve formative work as a leader, strengthening capability and ensuring judgement deepens as efficiency rises.

The model improves governance by offering a clear map of impact. You can link your AI initiative pipeline (developed through the previous chapters) to the four zones and see how each decision affects experience, trust and capacity. You can spot when automation is outpacing capability and where augmentation requires investment. You can identify the parts of the organisation where empathy must remain untouched because trust is fragile. In doing so, governance shifts from policing to guidance.

Building alignment and sustaining discipline

Used at scale, the Intelligent Work Model becomes shared language. Product, engineering, HR, operations and risk begin working from the same view of work. Functions stop pursuing isolated AI agendas, duplication falls and coherence rises. Decision-making accelerates because everyone is reading from the same map.

The model's power lies in its structure. It keeps you honest about where value sits for your organisation. It ensures automation strengthens capability rather than hollowing it out. It ensures augmentation expands judgement rather than bypassing it. It ensures empathy remains the anchor of trust and the foundation of long-term resilience.

Above all, the model brings clarity. You can stop asking where to begin as a leader and start asking what the work demands. You can stop trying to automate everything and start targeting the tasks that deliver meaningful impact. You can stop worrying about losing control and start shaping the future of work with intention.

That is the promise of the Intelligent Work Model. It does not guarantee success but it does guarantee focus. It aligns technology with human value and creates the conditions for AI to compound rather than fragment. It turns intelligent work from an abstract ambition into a practical direction of travel.

Application: Where the problem has the budget

One of the most frequent questions clients ask me is disarmingly simple: where should we begin? It usually arrives late in the conversation, right after a spirited debate about strategy, risk and whether anyone is allowed to use an AI tool without three forms, two approvals and a ceremonial blessing from Legal.

The leaders I talk to are often paralysed. On one hand, they can see the transformative potential of AI. They can see the big bets – the kind that change cost curves, compress cycle times and reshape customer experience. But those projects feel complex and high risk. They touch core systems, trigger governance and demand decisions. They involve the words 'operating model', which is usually where the room goes quiet.

On the other hand, leaders can see a heap of quick wins. Little automations, simple copilots and faster reporting all feel safe, but leaders worry they are just productivity snacks. They might be nice in the moment, but are not enough to change the business.

Clouding the whole program is the elephant in the room. People are quietly watching. They may not say much in meetings, but you can feel it in the questions they do not ask. What does this mean for me? What happens to my role? Am I about to be automated out of existence by someone who cannot open a PDF without assistance?

This is the moment when most organisations do one of two things. They either overreach and launch a dozen initiatives at once, hoping something sticks, or they freeze and tell themselves they will return to it once the market is clearer. Both options are expensive. One burns money while the other burns time. Neither builds trust.

I was discussing this exact mess with Scott Thomson, former head of Google Innovation in Australia, and he gave me the most useful piece of advice I have heard in corporate innovation. He said, 'Jamie, it's easy. The problem has the budget'.

Scott's approach is elegant because it replaces ambition with discipline. It is a hack in the best sense. Why chase new funding and face resistance when the answer is already sitting in the P&L, quietly eating it?

Organisations are riddled with problems waiting to be solved. These aren't the interesting kind of problems that make for a great keynote, but the annoying kind. The problems that clog workflow, drain capacity and force good people to do bad work. The genius in Scott's point is that high-pain problems are almost always high-value problems. If they were not valuable, nobody would be paying for them. Yet most organisations are paying for them every day. They're paying in overtime, churn, rework, contractors, missed deadlines and customers who do not come back.

That means these problems self-fund. You are not asking your organisation to bet on a speculative idea, but offering to stop an existing leak.

A second benefit also comes with this, and it matters just as much. High-pain problems are a pain in the arse, which means people are motivated to solve them. Rather than resisting your AI initiative, they welcome you. The enemy of my enemy is my friend, so to speak. The teams living with the pain become your greatest allies. They show up, provide data and tolerate the messiness of change because the current state is worse. They become the foundational core of your AI champions.

And that is how the flywheel starts. **You win by using AI to solve high-value, high-pain problems that are already funded. Then you win again by reducing fear and increasing workforce support because people can see the intent.** You offer relief, not replacement; progress, not panic. Thanks, Scott.

So, with 'the problem has the budget' in mind, here are four target-rich areas where I have repeatedly seen organisations find traction quickly and safely.

Headcount pain

Every organisation has departments that cannot hire fast enough. Some roles remain open for months. Others churn faster than they can be filled. As a leader, you might assume this is a talent problem. While sometimes it is, more often it reflects structural overload. Simply more work is available than people. It's a supply or demand problem but, either way, it's high-value pain. And we love solving high-value pain with AI.

This is where automation has the cleanest entry. Automating open headcount is not about removing jobs but creating relief. It is about giving stretched teams a margin of capacity that does not depend on more recruitment cycles. HR, finance and operations sit at the centre of this pressure. The awkward but useful reality is that most back-office functions already know their headcount is capped, even if nobody has put it in writing. Priority roles will always flow to revenue-generating and customer-facing teams. The rest are expected to cope. That is why AI automation and augmentation in the back office are almost always met with relief rather than resistance. They do not threaten identity. Instead, they reduce load and give teams breathing room in parts of the organisation that are permanently asked to do more with less.

AI can absorb the tasks that create that vulnerability. It can stabilise workflows, reduce backlog and create elasticity. This matters because the alternative is fatigue. Teams work harder, leaders patch with contractors and costs rise without increasing capability. When AI is aimed at funded headcount gaps, it proves its value quickly. It removes pain that people already understand.

Customer friction

Next, ask where customers feel the most pain. These are the moments where impatience grows, expectations strain and loyalty erodes. AI can improve responsiveness, personalisation and consistency across journeys that have become too manual to scale. The signals of these pain points are easy to spot, and include long wait times, repeated contacts, complex handovers and complaints that feel unnervingly similar.

The goal here is not to remove humans but friction. AI helps by handling first responses, guiding customers through predictable paths and surfacing the information that matters. It removes the repetitive interactions that exhaust frontline staff and leave customers frustrated. When done with intention, it improves the experience on both sides. Customers feel progress while teams feel supported. As a leader, you see the shift in reduced churn, higher satisfaction and lower operational drag.

The payoff is practical, reducing firefighting and increasing value-creating work. When customers stop spending energy navigating your processes, they start spending energy with your product.

Performance gaps

Performance gaps are the parts of the business where key metrics lag behind expectations. They are often well understood but under-addressed because the fixes feel labour intensive. Meanwhile, conversion falls short, cycle times stretch, forecast accuracy wavers and error rates climb.

These gaps are some of the most reliable places to apply AI. Predictive models, improved workflows and targeted copilots can impact these numbers quickly. They take the patterns hiding in the data and turn them into timely action. The transformation is visible and measurable. Leadership attention follows because the improvement lands squarely on the scoreboard.

Fixing what is already monitored is one of the fastest ways to build credibility. People do not need to imagine the value. They can see it. They can feel the work becoming faster, cleaner and more predictable. This quietens scepticism and anchors AI in real operational benefit.

Regulation and compliance

Finally, look at regulated areas not as burdens but strategic opportunities. Compliance teams spend significant time on documentation, auditing and monitoring. These activities require accuracy and consistency. They are critical to trust, yet they drain capacity from other parts of the organisation.

AI can transform these obligations. It can detect anomalies early, surface exceptions faster and generate the documentation that audits demand. It reduces human error and increases the reliability of oversight. This turns compliance from a cost centre into a stabiliser. When AI augments the routine elements, experts can focus on interpretation and judgement rather than administration.

In sectors where trust determines legitimacy, this shift matters. Leaders can meet obligations with more confidence. Regulators see fewer surprises. Customers feel safer. This is one of the few areas where risk reduction, efficiency and credibility rise together.

Building momentum through sequenced wins

Begin in any of these four areas of pain and the path forward becomes clearer. Each early win funds the next. Pressure eases in one part of the organisation, and the relief and momentum spills over into others. You start to see outcomes as a leader, not promises. Employees feel support, not surveillance. Employees feel support, not scrutiny. Your organisation as a whole starts to breathe a little easier.

Momentum matters because AI is not a single leap. It is a rhythm. Starting where the problem has the budget creates a self-funding loop. It turns AI from a cost into an engine. It proves that intelligent work is not about chasing novelty but resolving the pressure points that everyone already recognises.

The flywheel forms quietly, creating a stabilised workflow, shorter customer queue, more predictable metrics and smoother audits. Each improvement builds trust. Trust creates permission. Permission creates ambition.

This is how AI shifts from scattered projects to a coherent program. It starts in the places most people try last: the places that are unglamorous and painful, but funded. The places everyone complains about but nobody thinks to transform. These are the real gateways to intelligent work.

Start there and the rest follows.

Playbook: The self-funding AI strategy

AI transformation works best when it is sequenced, not simultaneous. The aim is to build a rhythm that produces early wins, protects trust and grows capability without overwhelming the organisation. When the order is right, value compounds.

Here's how:

1. **Automate first to create capacity:** Start with high expertise, low judgement work. These tasks produce quick, visible returns and face the least cultural resistance. They free stretched teams from load and show that AI can remove effort without removing value.
2. **Augment next to scale experience:** Use the time and headroom automation creates. Give your most experienced people the tools that multiply their judgement. Augmentation using AI deepens capability and strengthens the parts of the organisation that still rely on interpretation, nuance and consequence.
3. **Protect empathy where trust drives value:** Identify the roles and tasks in your organisation where human connection is the differentiator. Coaching, negotiation and leadership depend on credibility. Keep people at the centre and use AI only to support at the edges. Trust is built here, not automated.
4. **Turn savings into sponsorship:** Ring fence the gains from automation and reinvest them into augmentation. Self-funding programs grow faster because each improvement pays for the next.
5. **Govern for rhythm, not hype:** Work in 90-day cycles. Measure outcomes, recalibrate and repeat. Consistency outperforms enthusiasm. Momentum becomes the operating system.

The provocation: Follow the money, not the hype

Every company is somewhere on the AI curve, yet few see where the money is actually going. The budget already knows.

Leaders keep searching for new use cases while overlooking the ones their P&L is already shouting about. AI does not need a moonshot. It needs a mandate. Begin where the problem already has a budget, and let proof fund ambition. Start with the pressure points that already hurt, the ones people mention in corridor conversations, the ones that quietly stall progress. These areas do not need a pitch deck. They need relief. They are already paying for a solution. They are asking for help without using the words.

But money is only half the story. The other half is judgement. AI is not dangerous because it is powerful. It is dangerous because it is easy. Put it in the wrong hands and you get confident error at scale. Put it in the right hands and you get leverage. It's the same tool, but a different outcome.

Your opportunity?

- Automate the routine.
- Augment the experienced.
- Protect empathy where trust is the product.

Because the real measure of progress is not how much work you replace, but how much value you release.

So, look at your balance sheet and not your backlog. The future of intelligent work is already funded. The only question is whether you will notice.

What's next

Making the right choices about automation and augmentation is only the beginning. Those choices create momentum, but momentum does not turn into impact on its own. Most organisations stall in the gap between intention and execution, collecting pilots, steering committees and slide decks as proof they are 'doing AI'. The next chapter is about closing that gap with a practice, not a program. It shows how to build transformation muscle through a living portfolio of bets, four-week innovation sprints, and clear prototype-to-pilot-to-production lanes that keep learning honest and progress safe. If this chapter helped you put the tools in the right hands, the next shows you how to build the rhythm that keeps those hands moving.

CHAPTER 7

From intent to impact

I really love what I do. More importantly, I genuinely enjoy the people I do it with. My team and I spend an unreasonable amount of time taking the piss out of each other, which I have come to believe is a reliable indicator of psychological safety. If no-one is mocking you, something is wrong.

When my first few books were published, a familiar question started to appear at dinners and lunches, usually delivered with a cheeky grin. 'So', people would ask, 'who actually wrote it?' Sometimes they skipped the preamble and went straight to, 'Ghostwriter, yeah?'

I get a similar reaction when I talk with aspiring authors. They lean in, lower their voice and ask for the secret. How do you run a busy consulting practice, work with boards, travel constantly, and still punch out a book every 12 to 18 months? They are expecting some monk-like routine, a secluded cabin or at least a dramatic revelation.

The answer always disappoints them. I just write the book – not in a poetic sense; literally. I aim for 40,000 words and around ten chapters, meaning 4000 words per chapter. Write 1000 words a day and you can have a very rough first draft in six weeks. You're not waiting for the lightning bolt or muse. You're just turning up and typing, even when the words are average and the coffee is doing most of the heavy lifting.

Is it a bit more complicated than that? Of course. The process also includes editing, considering structure, thinking, rewriting, swearing at yourself – and cursing the developer who produced the abomination known as Microsoft Word. But the core idea holds. Progress comes from repetition, not inspiration. Momentum beats motivation every time.

When I look back, an uncomfortable number of the things I am proudest of in my life were built this way. They were achieved not through heroic effort, but through small, almost boring targets, ground out with a level of discipline that never looks impressive from the outside. Nothing is glamorous about writing 1000 words on a Tuesday morning at 5 am – or going to the gym when you would rather not, or doing the next sensible thing instead of the exciting one.

But this approach is why, when it came to figuring out how organisations should actually make progress with AI, I defaulted to the same pattern. I didn't look at grand plans, perfect roadmaps or six-month pilots that exhaust everyone and convince leadership that transformation is hard. I simply looked for a system that forces movement through small bets, clear questions and short cycles. I looked for enough structure to stay safe, and enough pace to stay honest.

This chapter is about that idea. It's about the idea that transformation, like writing a book or building muscle, is not a breakthrough event. It is a practice. You do not get strong by thinking about the gym. You do not get fluent by talking about learning a language. And you do not build AI capability by admiring it from a distance.

You build it by turning up, doing the work, and repeating the loop until progress stops feeling fragile and starts feeling normal.

That is the muscle we are here to build.

The discipline that makes AI work

Transformation is no longer a project to be delivered. It is a practice that rewards consistency rather than scale. Each cycle through an experiment, a decision or a lesson strengthens the organisation. Progress compounds through movement, not through plans.

That discipline rests on three ideas:

1. a living portfolio of AI bets that evolves with learning
2. four-week innovation sprints that convert possibilities into proven use cases
3. clear prototype, pilot and production workflows that provide enough structure to move from idea to impact without chaos.

The idea is simple. **Building transformation muscle is a lot like building physical muscle. It takes repetition, resistance and rhythm.** Lift a weight once and nothing happens. Lift it again and again, and you grow stronger. Use good form, and you avoid injury. Your organisation is no different.

AI raises the stakes, multiplying both opportunity and risk. Leaders look out and see new possibilities everywhere. Teams feel swamped by choices. Governance tries to keep up. People worry about making the wrong move. Progress does not stall because the technology is confusing, but because decision-making gets overloaded.

The transformation system described here tackles that overload head-on. It gives you as a leader a repeatable way to prioritise, test, learn and move. It aligns with the models and guardrails you have already met through this book. It brings together strategy, structure and behaviour so your organisation can build capability as it delivers value.

The goal is simple: to create a way of working that keeps you moving, even after the novelty of AI fades. This is a way of working that turns momentum into muscle, and can grow with the demands of intelligent work.

Why now: Standing in the middle of a storm

The real challenge for leaders is not only how fast things are changing, but also how much. Disruption does not come in a single wave but in layers, bringing new tools, new behaviours and new expectations. Each layer might be manageable on its own, but together they can overwhelm. This is disruption density: many small changes piling up faster than anyone can absorb.

AI turns up the volume on this density. Suddenly, every team can spot ten new use cases before lunch. Executives dream up new workflows. Lists of opportunities grow longer by the day. This is an environment bursting with potential but short on clarity. The result is familiar: decision fatigue sets in, coordination slips and the organisation becomes a resting place for ideas that never made it off the slide deck.

But density is only part of the story. Another force is at work: evidence now matters more than opinion. AI takes away the old excuses, because experiments are cheap. Leaders do not need committees to guess at value. They can see it, measure it and test it in days. The organisations that thrive treat evidence as currency. They run small, focused experiments and swap forecasts for real results. They build confidence with working prototypes, not with theatre.

The third force is emotional. AI is as much a psychological disruption as a technical one. People worry about relevance, identity and whether they will still matter in the next version of the organisation. Traditional training and communication programs do not solve this. What does is participation. When teams build, test and play with AI in short, safe cycles, morale rises. Anxiety falls. Literacy grows. People stop fearing the technology and start shaping it.

Put these forces together, and a simple truth emerges. **Organisations rarely fail for lack of ideas. They fail because they do not have a structure that keeps people learning, deciding and adapting together.** They wait for clarity before acting when, in fact, action is what brings clarity.

You cannot:

- plan your way out of disruption density
- communicate your way out of fear
- delegate your way into AI literacy.

You build your way out.

The framework: The AI innovation sprint

Organisations do not develop AI capability by planning alone. They build it by running short, focused cycles that turn possibility into evidence, and evidence into momentum. The AI innovation sprint is the engine that makes this possible. It is the simplest, safest way to turn strategy into something you can see and touch.

An innovation sprint is a four-week, design-led experiment. It mirrors 'double diamond' design thinking: diverging to understand the problem, converging to define it, diverging again to explore solutions and converging finally to test what works. This sprint is fast enough to remove excuses and structured enough to avoid chaos. It is the organisational equivalent of a laboratory; a place where ideas can be explored, challenged and evolved without the burden of a full project behind them.

The goal is not perfection but clarity. Clarity about whether an idea deserves more investment, about the shape of the solution, about the capabilities required to take it further, and about value, risk and feasibility. Clarity that is earned, not assumed.

The sprint has four phases: discover and define, design and assemble, test and decide, assess and adjust. Each phase has its own output, rhythm and form of value. Together, they create a cycle that builds skill, confidence and literacy as it builds evidence.

The AI innovation sprint is the core discipline required to thrive in an AI-native world.

Why sprints

Sprints are the engine that turns ideas into evidence. AI introduces an abundance of possibility, prompting too many ideas, too many tools and too many competing priorities. Without a disciplined way of funnelling this noise into structured learning, organisations stall. They overanalyse, waiting for alignment and certainty. They wait for someone else to move first.

A sprint breaks this paralysis by doing three things at once.

First, it reduces scope. The four-week timeframe forces focus and eliminates complexity. It removes the temptation to overbuild. Second, the sprint produces evidence, returning a clear view of feasibility, value and risk. It replaces speculation with data and gives leaders something solid to act on. Lastly, it builds capability. People learn by doing. They build literacy, confidence and judgement. They stop fearing the technology and start shaping it.

This is how transformation muscle grows. You do the work. You find the rhythm. You let repetition turn knowledge into skill.

Understanding the qualities of an AI innovation sprint

An AI innovation sprint is a short, focused exploration of a single AI opportunity. It is not a project, proof of concept or a pilot. It is a controlled experiment designed to generate clarity and evidence.

Five qualities define a sprint:

1. **It has a single question:** What is the one thing we need to prove or disprove in four weeks?
2. **It focuses on problems, not solutions:** The work starts by looking for friction, failure points and what people

actually want to achieve. The solution grows out of insight, not assumption.

3. **It is built on design thinking:** Explore the problem, define it clearly, look at different ways to solve it, and then pick and test the simplest approach that might work.
4. **It uses AI as a collaborator:** Foundation models, agents, vibe-coded prototypes, simulation tools and synthetic data accelerate every step.
5. **It ends with a decision:** Go, hold or no-go. No ambiguity.

This structure means every sprint adds value, even if the answer is no. Your organisation learns and your team grows. The backlog gets smarter. Future decisions come more easily.

How an AI innovation sprint works

As shown in the figure opposite, the sprint is delivered over four tightly defined phases.

Phase 1: Discover and define

Find the real problem and make it small.

The aim here is to understand the problem before trying to solve it. Most teams skip this step. They rush to ideas, bring solutions to meetings and assume they already know what is wrong. That is how four weeks slip away. The sprint starts by slowing down just enough to see the work clearly.

Your team investigates the problem from the user's perspective. They run interviews, watch workflows, review data, and map friction and failure points. AI accelerates the analysis, generating interview guides, clustering notes, surfacing themes and synthesising patterns, but the interpretation remains human. Technology can summarise. Only people can judge.

4-week AI innovation sprint

Discover and define

Purpose: Agree the problem, the user and what success looks like.

Activities:
- Pick an AI use case and frame it clearly.
- Map the current journey/process in a few steps and mark the pain points.
- Write simple success measures, for example time saved or quality uplift.
- Sketch how we might solve it using today's tools before inventing new ones.

Outputs:
- One-page brief with the question, user, success measure and constraints.
- Short plan for the next two weeks.

Typical tools: Digital whiteboard, quick user chats, simple worksheets.

Design and assemble

Purpose: Build the smallest working demo that can prove or disprove the idea.

Activities:
- Choose lightweight tools first, configure rather than code where possible.
- Create a safe test set with synthetic or sample data if live data is not ready.
- Assemble a thin end-to-end path so a real task can be run start to finish.
- Label any gaps clearly so we know what is mocked and what is real.

Outputs:
- A small working demo that runs on test data.
- A test plan that states what we will measure and how.

Possible forms: Clickable prototype, prototype agent, basic dashboard, or a feasibility study if a demo is not yet sensible.

Test and decide

Purpose: Get evidence and make a clear decision.

Activities:
- Put the demo in front of real users where safe or run it with the sprint team.
- Capture simple measures, for example time taken, error rates, useful insights.
- Collect reactions from users in their own words.
- Compare results to the success measure and decide go or hold or kill.

Outputs:
- Results pack with data, what we learned and visible risks.
- Decision record with the next step, for example scale plan, refine and retest, or stop and capture learning.

Assess and adjust

Purpose: Keep the momentum, improve the way we work and set up the next sprint.

Activities:
- Short review of what helped and what slowed us down.
- Update and reprioritise the AI use case list if needed.
- Confirm the next AI use case and project lead.

Outputs:
- Updated delivery plan and a one-page plan for the next sprint.

Once the landscape is clear, the team comes together. They distil everything into a single sentence that defines the problem. They pick three signs of success. They note the constraints that will matter later: data, systems, adoption risks, compliance and policy. All of this goes into a one-page brief that explains why this matters now.

This brief anchors the sprint. It keeps your team together, stops scope from drifting and makes sure you are solving something that matters.

Primary output: A one-page problem brief that defines the user, the problem, the success indicators and the constraints.

When the problem is defined well, the rest of the sprint falls into place.

Phase 2: Design and assemble

Build the simplest thing that teaches you the most.

This phase turns insight into possibility. The team shifts from understanding the problem to exploring how AI might address it. They sketch workflows, storyboard user journeys and test different model prompts. They examine decision points, edge cases and alternative approaches. They assemble lightweight prototypes: an agent, a decision-support tool, a generative content flow, a RAG-powered search or a simple simulation. The aim is not to impress but to learn.

AI accelerates every part of this phase. It generates screens, mock-ups and personas. It synthesises design variants, adjusts prompts and forecasts likely failure points. It gives the team options, not answers.

The discipline in this phase is to keep things light. Build the smallest version that is good enough to test. Your team can think of this as a sketch with substance or a prototype with bite. It should be something real enough to spark judgement and reveal risk.

Two rules keep the work honest during this phase:

- Keep it lightweight.
- Keep it real.

Build too much, and you hide the flaws and waste time. Build too little, and you learn nothing. The real skill is in the middle: build just enough to show value, feasibility and risk.

Primary output: A lightweight working prototype that is testable against the success indicators defined in phase 1.

This prototype is not the product. It is your hypothesis, made tangible.

Phase 3: Test and decide

Put it in real hands. Watch what happens.

This is where the sprint gets real. The prototype leaves the team and lands with the people who would actually use it. It is not a polished, finished product, but the simplest version that lets people interact for real. The goal is to see how it behaves in the wild, and how people respond when the idea is no longer just a theory.

Testing is deliberately practical. Users try it. They comment, hesitate and ask questions. They push its edges. They reveal expectations and anxieties that never show up in workshops. These reactions matter as much as the numbers, because AI succeeds only when people trust it, understand it and choose to adopt it.

The team observes the interactions closely. They measure how long tasks take, where the prototype gets stuck and where it surprises people. They track accuracy, relevance and error rates. They note which prompts work and which ones fall apart. They watch for trust signals: moments when a user leans in, pulls back, delegates a decision or overrides one. The aim is to discover how the prototype fits into the real rhythm of work.

AI supports the process by analysing feedback, comparing versions, flagging anomalies and summarising common themes. But the judgement is human. Evidence is not a dashboard. It is behaviour.

At the end of the cycle, the team brings the findings to the sponsor and recommends one of three paths:

1. **Go:** The prototype created real value and people responded positively. Move to pilot.
2. **Hold:** The idea shows promise, but a dependency or risk must be resolved or retested before the next step.
3. **No-go:** The evidence does not justify further investment. The sprint has done its job by preventing waste.

The decision is clear because the evidence is lived, not imagined. This is where leaders get something rare in AI work: real insight into what will work in their own organisation, not someone else's.

Primary output: A go, hold or no-go decision supported by real user interaction and observable evidence.

This is the moment when theory becomes truth.

Phase 4: Assess and adjust

Turn what you learned into your next move.

The final phase closes the loop and turns activity into capability. This is where the team steps back from the prototype and asks what the sprint really taught them. Not in a bureaucratic way, but in a practical, honest sense. What was surprising? What was harder than expected? What worked well? How did users react? What does the evidence really say about what to do next?

The retrospective is not an afterthought. It is the moment where your organisation builds judgement. The team walks through the four weeks with a clear eye. They review the problem brief and revisit the success indicators. They examine whether the prototype revealed the right things. They discuss how the process felt, and capture risks and dependencies that surfaced along the way. They identify capability gaps that might need support.

The conversation is honest. This is where teams articulate what they would do differently next time. It is where they notice patterns across sprints and start to build a common language. AI helps by summarising notes, clustering insights and producing first-pass themes, but meaning is created by people. Reflection is a human competency.

The aim is not to celebrate or defend. The aim is to understand.

Once the insights are captured, the team updates the AI transformation backlog. They adjust priorities, scope or timing based on what the sprint revealed. They note what the next sprint should explore. They flag anything that needs escalation or support. They turn learning into action so momentum keeps building.

The loop closes only when the learning is banked, the backlog is updated and the next move is clear. This is how rhythm develops, transformation becomes repeatable and muscle forms.

Primary output: A structured retrospective that captures the key lessons and directly informs the next sprint and the wider transformation portfolio.

Reflection is not the end of the sprint. It is the foundation of the next one.

Why an AI innovation sprint works

The AI innovation sprint works because it aligns technology, behaviour and judgement in the following ways:

- It gives leaders evidence they can trust.
- It gives teams a safe space to experiment.
- It gives governance clarity.
- It gives the organisation a rhythm.

But more than anything, it gives people the ability to participate. And participation builds morale, literacy and confidence. The three things AI disruption quietly erodes.

A sprint is not a project. It is a practice. A practice that builds muscle, one loop at a time.

Application: Building the transformation engine

The AI innovation sprint is only powerful when it sits inside a deliberate, structured implementation path. On its own, a sprint is a four-week experiment. Placed inside the right system, it becomes the engine of an AI-native transformation. The implementation steps shown in the following figure, and expanded on in the following sections, outline how your organisation aligns direction, discovers opportunities, shapes the portfolio, runs sprints and then scales what works through safe technology lanes.

Strategic alignment and foundation (1)	Opportunity alignment and prioritisation (2)	Implementation and experimentation (3)
Sponsor alignment 1:1 with the executive sponsor to set goals, guardrails and success measures. Output: program brief and named project leads. **Kickoff workshop** Executive team session to introduce the program and sprint method. Output: shared understanding and agreed rhythm. **Blueprint workshop 1** Define key drivers, ambition and value levers. Output: AI Strategy Blueprint v0.1.	**Stakeholder interviews** 1:1 across the business to capture and score AI use cases. Output: first cut of AI use cases. **Sponsor review** Review long list with sponsor, select near-term candidates and confirm resourcing. Output: short list ready for exec discussion. **Blueprint workshop 2** Confirm initiatives, enablers and guardrails, then finalise plan. Output: signed blueprint and starter sprint plan. **Board briefing** Optional session to align the board on the AI journey, share core concepts and build intent.	**Run AI innovation sprints** Move prioritised AI use cases through a three-week AI innovation sprint to explore ideas, build a small working demo, and capture evidence in a safe-to-fail environment.
First month		Ongoing cadence

This is the practical sequence. One move sets up the next, and momentum builds through the loop.

Step 1: Align the organisation around the AI strategy blueprint

Everything starts with leadership alignment. Before running a single sprint, your executive team needs to share a clear sense of what they are trying to achieve and why. Creating an AI strategy blueprint, based on everything discussed through the earlier chapters of this book, gives structure to that alignment. It clarifies the North Star for the next 12 to 18 months and shows where the organisation wants to build its moats (refer to chapter 5). It then defines the balance of initiatives across optimise, accelerate and transform (covered in more detail in the next chapter).

This step also embeds the automation envelope from chapter 3, outlining what can be automated safely, where judgement must be preserved, and where empathy and trust is non-negotiable. Alignment is not about ambition but shared intent. Without this clarity, sprints become directionless. With it, they accelerate the strategy.

Step 2: Explore the work and identify real opportunities

Once direction is set, the next move is discovery. This is where you step into the work itself. As leader, you commission a short, intense look at how your organisation really works today. This might mean interviews, workflow walkthroughs, customer journey mapping, friction audits and listening to frontline staff. AI can help cluster notes and spot patterns, but meaning comes from people.

The result is a long, unfiltered list of opportunities grounded in lived experience, not just imagination. These opportunities naturally fall into the three horizons covered in the next chapter:

1. **Optimise:** Where repetitive work, delays or errors create avoidable cost.
2. **Accelerate:** Where AI can enhance products, services or expert decision-making.
3. **Transform:** Where new value propositions, business models or operating models may emerge.

The point of this step is breadth. You cannot prioritise what you have not seen.

Step 3: Shape and sharpen the AI transformation portfolio

Discovery brings volume. The portfolio gives it shape. As leader, you can now refine each opportunity into a short, clear statement: the problem, the user, the value, the constraint and the learning potential. This discipline keeps the portfolio grounded.

Opportunities are then evaluated through four lenses:

1. **Value:** Does it solve something meaningful?
2. **Feasibility:** Can it be explored without an unrealistic technical burden?
3. **Strategic fit:** Does it align with the North Star?
4. **Learning value:** Does it build the capability the organisation needs next?

The portfolio becomes the transformation plan. It is not a roadmap frozen in PowerPoint, but a live set of bets your organisation will test through sprints.

Step 4: Begin running AI innovation sprints

The portfolio tells you what to explore. The sprint tells you what is real. Each sprint takes one opportunity and gives it four weeks of focused attention. It follows the double diamond rhythm already discussed: explore the problem, define it clearly, look at solutions and then test the simplest prototype that can show evidence.

This is where capability starts to grow. People learn how AI behaves. They learn to shape prompts, test assumptions, interpret results and spot failure signals. They see value in the hands of real users. Most importantly, they feel forward movement. They stop waiting and start doing.

As sprints begin to run sequentially, or in parallel in more mature teams, your organisation builds its transformation muscle. **Each loop produces more evidence, each decision becomes sharper and each lesson compounds.**

Step 5: Move from prototype to pilot to production

Sprints create evidence, but evidence only matters when it moves safely into the real world. That is why every organisation needs three technology lanes:

1. **Prototype is speed:** This lane is all about lightweight tools, synthetic data and minimal risk. This is where sprints live. You learn quickly, cheaply and safely.
2. **Pilot is validation:** The solution is integrated into a real workflow with real users under controlled conditions. Integration is partial. Governance tightens. You and your team see how the idea behaves in your environment rather than in theory.

3. **Production is scale:** This lane is about full integration, observability, assurance, identity and policy. This is where AI becomes part of the organisational spine.

Moving between lanes is earned. A sprint gives a go decision. A pilot validates the behaviour. Production locks in stability. Nothing moves forward on enthusiasm alone. This step-by-step path protects trust and ensures you scale ideas that are ready. It keeps innovation safe, without slowing it down.

Step 6: Establish the organisational rhythm

Once sprints and lanes are moving, the final step is cadence. Cadence stops drift and turns experimentation into muscle. You and your leadership team review the portfolio every quarter. Sponsors review sprint outcomes every month. Sprint teams keep their rhythm every week. This creates a shared tempo across your organisation.

As this rhythm strengthens, AI literacy increases, decision-making accelerates and morale stabilises. People stop fearing disruption when they participate in shaping it. Teams feel the movement. Leadership sees the momentum. Your organisation develops reflexes that do not rely on heroics.

This is how AI transformation becomes sustainable.

Not by planning harder, but by working in loops, learning in public and treating movement as a practice.

Playbook: The transformation engine in five moves

The organisations that thrive are the ones that treat movement as a practice, not a project. Here's how:

1. **Start with a shared North Star:** Agree on why AI matters and what your organisation is trying to achieve in the next 12 to 18 months. When leaders align early, every sprint becomes an accelerator, not an argument.
2. **Build the portfolio before you build the prototype:** Explore the work, map pain and listen to users. Capture every viable opportunity across optimise, accelerate and transform. Shape each one into a thin, readable statement. Only then decide what to test first.
3. **Run AI innovation sprints as the default learning loop:** Give each opportunity four weeks of structured attention using the double diamond approach. Put prototypes in real hands. Make decisions based on evidence, not enthusiasm. Keep the rhythm tight.
4. **Move ideas through the three lanes:** Use the prototype lane for exploration, pilot for validation and production for scale. Nothing jumps the queue. Progress is earned through evidence. This protects trust and prevents costly missteps.
5. **Establish a transformation cadence:** Use quarterly portfolio reviews, monthly sprint decisions and a weekly sprint rhythm. Cadence builds confidence. Confidence builds capability. Capability builds momentum.

The provocation: Stop planning and start proving

AI will not remake your organisation in one dramatic leap. It will do it in quiet, repeatable, disciplined loops. The kind of loops that build capability the same way muscle grows: through resistance, recovery and rhythm.

Most organisations never make this shift. They wait for clarity and certainty. They wait for a perfect roadmap that never arrives. While they wait, competitors learn in public. They run small experiments, test assumptions, collect lessons and build confidence one sprint at a time.

The real divide is no longer between organisations that understand AI and those that do not. It is between the organisations that practise and the ones that perform. One treats transformation as theatre. The other treats it as work. One talks about innovation. The other builds it, tests it and adjusts it before lunch.

The uncomfortable truth is that you cannot think your way into this future. You have to move your way into it. You have to replace 'prediction' with 'evidence'. You have to build a system that keeps you learning even when the noise is loud and the path is unclear. You have to create a rhythm that outlasts enthusiasm.

If you do that, your organisation becomes steadier, braver and more capable of absorbing change without losing its footing. Your people stop fearing the technology because they are part of shaping it. Your leaders stop waiting for perfect information because they trust the loop.

AI rewards motion, not mastery. The companies that win will not be the ones with the biggest plans, but the ones with the strongest reflexes.

So ask yourself the only question that matters now. If you had to prove your next idea in four weeks, how would you begin tomorrow?

What's next

Building transformation muscle gives your organisation the ability to move. But movement alone does not solve the hardest problem leaders now face. AI forces you to change while the business is still running. You must improve today's operations even as tomorrow's model takes shape, often under very different assumptions. The next chapter tackles that tension head-on. It explores how leaders run the core business at speed while simultaneously building what comes next, without starving either of attention or credibility. Using the simple frame of trains and planes, it shows when to optimise, when to break away and how to manage disruption without derailing the organisation that still pays the bills.

Trains, planes and disruption

Imagine you run a railway. You lay track across vast distances. You build stations, assemble engines, hire drivers and manage timetables. You worry about signalling, maintenance windows and peak-hour flow. Over time, the system settles into a rhythm. Small improvements compound, bottlenecks smooth out and delays become rare.

Your teams know the network intimately. Engineers recognise faults by sound alone. Station managers can predict congestion before it appears. Dispatchers adjust schedules by instinct. Reliability becomes your advantage. Precision becomes your culture. The organisation feels calm because the system is understood.

Then flight arrives.

At first, it looks irrelevant. The strange winged machines have unstable controls and limited reach. They're fragile and impractical. They carry few passengers and break often. They feel like toys for enthusiasts, not serious infrastructure. From the safety of the rails, it is easy to dismiss them.

But the technology improves. Controls stabilise and engines become reliable. Routes expand, safety rises and travel times collapse. Journeys that once took days now take hours. The comparison shifts quietly. What looked novel begins to look inevitable.

Customers notice first. They start asking different questions and expecting different outcomes. Your teams feel the change second-hand, through demand patterns that no longer behave as predicted. The industry that once rewarded optimisation is suddenly being outpaced by possibility.

Now you have a decision to make. You can double-down on what you know and borrow the technology of flight to build faster trains. You can refine the system, automate operations and reduce cost. You can improve punctuality and scale efficiency. These trains are extraordinary machines. And for many journeys, they remain the right answer. If your model still fits the world, modernising it can deliver enormous value.

Or you can decide you are not in the railway business, but the transportation business – and start building planes. That path is different. It requires new skills, new economics and new tolerances for risk. One system depends on rails and schedules. The other depends on learning. One values control while the other rewards exploration. Try to run both with the same teams, the same measures and the same assumptions and eventually one will cripple the other.

This is where many organisations now find themselves with AI.

Some can modernise their railway, building faster, smarter and more automated trains to carry them forward for years. Others face a deeper shift. Their passengers have already left the platform. In those cases, the question is no longer whether to fly, but how to do it before the runway disappears.

Tracks or wings?

This chapter is about the disruptive impact of AI, knowing that impact on your business model, and what it takes to run two different kinds of change at once if the world demands it. AI has not rewritten every business model, but it has rewritten the economics of speed, cost and possibility. Some organisations can upgrade what they already have. Others need to build a completely new business model. The hard part is working out which camp your organisation is in before the market decides for you.

The trap is to treat all disruptive change as the same. When every initiative is labelled transformation, the core business always wins. It wins because it is familiar. It wins because it has revenue attached. It wins because its risks are known and its politics are predictable. Yet if the underlying business model is being outpaced, improving the core only buys time.

The mechanism for solving this problem is initiating a dual transformation, and it gives you as a leader a method of managing this tension without tearing your organisation apart. Strengthen what must endure. Build what might replace it. Keep both moving, but never at the same speed, with the same team or under the same rules. This is a model and discipline for leaders facing markets where the past no longer guarantees the future.

The basic argument is simple. **AI increases disruptive pressure. It forces a sharper distinction between improvement and invention.** It demands that leaders decide whether they are running a railway, an airline or something in between. In this chapter, I outline how to diagnose the disruption, choose the right path and manage the organisational split that follows. The goal is not harmony but coherence, with enough stability to protect what works and enough ambition to build what comes next.

Why now: The pressure front

As I mentioned in chapter 4, I have spent much of my career inside organisations that disrupted traditional industries and large entrenched players. These organisations have included Red Hat (open-source software), Salesforce.com (software as a service) and realestate.com.au (online property classifieds). What fascinated me was never the technology itself but the response. Incumbents rarely ignore disruption. They recognise it and discuss it. They approve a program. But then they try to solve it using the same teams, the same measures and the same instincts that made them successful in the first place. That works when the challenge is optimisation. It fails when the challenge is reinvention.

A lot of people tell the Amazon story as if it is simply about being first. Yes, Amazon sold books online. But others copied them, and some even did it quickly. Barnes & Noble had an online bookstore too. The difference was not the website but the company. Amazon was a native e-commerce business. E-commerce was in its DNA, in who it hired, how it built systems, how it measured performance and how it made decisions.

That distinction matters because it is now repeating. In many sectors, simply adding AI to the existing business will not be enough, especially for industries that sell expertise as the product. AI-native organisations will not just use the tools. They will be structured around them. They will build operating rhythm, capabilities and decision rights that assume AI is always present. That is why timing feels so brutal.

AI is compressing time and disrupting industries in the following ways:

- Strategy cycles that once spanned years now reset quarterly.
- A finance team can close its books in minutes.
- A marketing team can generate creative material faster than compliance can approve it.
- Procurement can be outpaced by a model that learns prices in real time.

The shelf life of competitive advantage has shrunk, but not every industry feels the same pain. Stable industries – for example, heavy manufacturing, utilities and logistics – can use AI to strengthen what they already do. For them, transformation is about faster trains, not building an airline. Disrupted sectors such as media, consulting and professional services, however, are watching their business models collapse. For them, the choice is existential. They need to act now.

Clayton Christensen called this environment the 'innovator's dilemma': success breeds inertia, and incumbents become prisoners of their own excellence. In *Dual Transformation*, Scott Anthony, Clark Gilbert and Mark Johnson offered a way out: strengthen the existing business while building the new one. They labelled these streams 'Transformation A' and 'Transformation B'. I draw on this concept in this chapter but use a simpler distinction here: faster trains *and* planes. AI has made the model urgent again, but not universal. The real skill now lies in knowing which game you're playing.

The framework: Dual transformation

Before you start making plans, you need to answer one vital question: is AI changing how your business runs, or changing what your business is? The pace and shape of disruption in your industry will determine your next move. Some sectors face gradual pressure. Others are already standing on ground that is shifting beneath them. Knowing the difference is what decides whether you invest in faster trains or whether you must build an airline.

Most leadership teams hesitate here. They react to the noise around AI. They see pilots, demos and prototypes and assume they must act quickly, without distinguishing urgency from inevitability. The real work begins with diagnosis, and I covered disruption velocity and organisational sensing in chapter 4. **What you need to know now is whether AI is changing the mechanics of work inside your current model, or eroding the economics of the model itself.** Without this clarity, you and your organisation can choose the wrong path, overreact, underreact or invest in capabilities that never convert into advantage.

The framework rests on a simple decision. If your business model remains sound, you stay on the rails and build faster trains. You use AI to optimise and accelerate the system you already run. If your business model is being outpaced, you must strengthen your railway while you build an airline. That is dual transformation. Once you commit to going down the airline path, a second decision is required: whether you build, buy or partner to create the new business you will need. Each path has different costs, risks and implications for leadership.

This structure gives you a disciplined way to decide how far you must go. It helps prevent unnecessary reinvention in stable markets and avoids cosmetic modernisation in disrupted ones. And it keeps your organisation focused on the real question: do we improve the system we have or build one that can take us somewhere the tracks will never reach?

Faster trains: Optimise and accelerate

Faster trains combine the two disciplines that strengthen your core business without changing its fundamental model. Optimise improves what already works by lifting productivity and efficiency, reducing cost and protecting margin. Accelerate uses AI to enhance your existing products and services, so the whole business creates more customer value and earns more revenue without changing what it fundamentally is. When disruption is limited, these disciplines can create enormous value. They let you and your organisation deliver margin improvement and customer uplift without rebuilding the business from scratch.

Optimise: Make the system lighter

Optimise is the work of modernising the everyday. It means automating predictable processes, compressing cycle times and removing friction. It means deploying AI copilots that support staff in real time. It means eliminating handoffs, tightening controls and simplifying decisions. It is incremental work in theory, but transformative in practice because it turns time into capacity and capacity into margin.

When your organisation commits to the optimise discipline, you create time, capacity and headroom. Every team becomes faster. Customers may not notice the mechanism, but they feel the reliability. Margins strengthen. The business becomes more resilient without changing its identity.

Accelerate: Redesign the way the business moves

Accelerate goes deeper. It looks at how work flows through the system and how your offerings show up in the market. It rewrites operating assumptions. It shifts the cadence of teams, governance and decisions. It redesigns the roles people play, the skills they need and the authority they hold. It begins to change the way your organisation thinks, not just how it executes.

Accelerate is where AI stretches its muscles. Products become smarter. Services become more personalised. Service becomes more responsive. The business moves from a steady pace to a quicker rhythm while improving customer experience and opening new revenue.

When faster trains are enough

Faster trains are enough when the fundamentals of your industry remain predictable. If customers still value reliability over radical new experiences, if competitors remain predictable, if economics remain grounded in physical assets, infrastructure or regulation, faster trains will take you far. You can modernise the system you already trust. You can deliver value, protect margins and compete aggressively without designing a completely new business model.

The only risk with this approach is complacency. Faster trains can create a false sense of safety. As a leader, you may mistake operational improvement for strategic durability. You may assume your organisation's model will always hold. Even in stable markets, however, expectations evolve. Costs change and new entrants arrive. Faster trains work best when leaders remain attentive to the heat beneath their platform, not blind to it.

Planes: When you must transform

Faster trains are not enough when the rules of the market start to change. Some organisations face pressures that the disciplines of optimise and accelerate cannot address alone. Customer expectations reset quickly. Competitors use AI to deliver outcomes that were previously unimaginable. Margins shrink and demand softens. The economics of the industry begin to reprice. This is particularly true for industries such as professional services that historically sold expertise as the product.

This is when you need planes. This is when you must transform.

Transform is the work of building a new business that does not rely on the constraints of the old one. It is where you define a new model, a new value proposition and a new way of delivering outcomes. The required skills are different. The economics and risks are different. Your organisation needs new rhythms, new structures and new behaviours. Transform is not improvement but invention.

Dual transformation: Trains and planes at once

When disruption is structural, you cannot abandon your existing business. It still carries passengers, generates cash and earns trust. And you cannot delay the new business either. It takes time to design a new business, time to launch and time to scale. This is why organisations that expect to be disrupted by AI must work on both businesses at once. They must strengthen the railway while building the airline.

This is dual transformation: strengthening the business you have while building the business you will need.

Dual transformation demands precision. The disciplines of optimise and accelerate must continue in your core business to maintain performance and free up cash and resources. Transform must explore, test and iterate at the edges of your organisation. Each side moves at a different pace. Each uses different measures of success. Each carries different risks.

Trying to run both under a single governance model is the fastest way to kill one or both. Dual transformation succeeds only when you as a leader treat them as two different games. One is about improvement, while the other is about discovery. One is about protecting value. The other is about creating it.

Every 90 days, you and your team need to recalibrate. Is the core business stable? How much runway does the transformation process need? What assumptions have shifted? What signals strengthened? This cadence keeps both sides moving in step, without forcing them into the same rhythm.

Transform pathways: Build, buy or partner

Once you commit to business model transformation, your focus also shifts from what to build to how to build it. This is where many organisations stall. They agree the existing model will not be enough, but then hesitate when they realise the next move is not a project. It is a capability decision. You need to choose how you will acquire the skills, operating rhythm and conviction required to make a new business real. In practical terms, this choice resolves into three paths: build your own AI-native business, buy one or partner with one.

Build: Designing your own AI-native business

Designing your own AI-native business from the ground up is the most demanding path. You and your organisation define new customer promises, new workflows and new economics. You build teams that think differently from your existing organisation. You create governance that rewards exploration.

The benefit is complete control. You shape the new business to your strategy. You embed the culture you want. You move at your chosen pace. But this is the hardest path because it stretches your organisation the furthest. Organisations built for optimisation often struggle with the ambiguity required to invent. Protecting the space for transform becomes your main job as leader.

Buy: Mergers and acquisitions

Acquiring a company that already is AI-native and has the capability embedded is your quickest path. You gain immediate access to skills, customers and technology. And if time pressure is high, buying can feel like the easiest and most direct route.

The biggest risk here, however, is price. AI-native companies are becoming more expensive as demand increases and supply stays constrained. Buying your way into the future may simply be unaffordable. Integration risk still matters, but economics are now the dominant constraint. You may end up owning a business you cannot justify, much less operate and scale.

Partner: Shared risk

Partnering is often the most pragmatic path when you need speed and learning without the full commitment of building or buying. In this option, you partner with AI-native firms to co-develop solutions, extend your offerings or enter new markets. You share risk, accelerate learning and reduce complexity.

Partnership works when you need speed but cannot justify the cost of an acquisition or the huge endeavour of building alone. It gives you optionality without overcommitting. The risk here is dependency. If you partner without building internal capability, your future becomes tied to someone else's trajectory. But with clear boundaries, partnership becomes a powerful accelerator.

Choosing the right path

The choice between enhancing your current business or building something new via dual transformation is your critical first decision. If disruption is limited, doubling down on the optimise and accelerate disciplines is a rational, effective and high-return strategy. In doing so, you strengthen the core business, improve the customer experience and protect margins. You create competitive advantage without the complexity of invention.

If disruption is structural, faster trains will not save you – optimise and accelerate will not be enough on their own. You must keep the current business stable while you build the next one.

Leaders often wait for certainty before choosing. But the current environment punishes delay. The question you face is not whether the path is perfect. It is whether the path matches the reality of your organisation's disruption, your capabilities and your appetite for risk.

When answered honestly, the choice becomes clear. Strengthen the core business. Build the next. And if transformation is inevitable, decide whether you build it yourself, buy your way out or partner to learn faster than you could alone.

Application: Turning direction into momentum

Dual transformation is not about working harder but about making deliberate strategic choices. The real danger is mistaking motion for momentum. Organisations drift when they fail to distinguish improvement from invention, or when they expect both to follow the same instincts, measures and rhythms. **Traditional core businesses behave one way. New AI-native business and operating models often behave differently. Trying to lead both with a single mindset is what turns transformation into a management nightmare.**

To make dual transformation work, you and your organisation must make five deliberate shifts. Each shift sounds simple, but none actually is. They cut through the habits that anchor teams to the familiar. They prevent the improvement work from cannibalising the invention work. And they stop the invention work from distracting the improvement work. Most importantly, they give your organisation a way to move at two speeds without tearing itself apart.

Label the lanes so everyone knows what game they are in

Language sets direction. When everything is called 'transformation', the existing business always wins. It wins because it is visible, it is funded and staff are comfortable with how to run it. The work of building the new future is slowly suffocated by legacy expectations and old reflexes.

One way to support the distinction is through language. You should name the different program lanes clearly and consistently. Call the work that strengthens and modernises the current business 'optimise' and 'accelerate'. These are the disciplines that build faster trains. Call the work of invention 'transform'. That is the discipline that builds planes. These labels are not decoration but alignment tools. They allow teams to behave differently without apology. They make it clear that improvement and invention play by different rules.

Teams should see the labels everywhere, including in agendas, planning documents, investment papers and board packs. Even small cues shape behaviour. When everyone knows which lane they are in, they stop arguing about whether new work is distracting the core business or suffocating the transformation work.

Redesign governance to match two speeds

The 'optimise and accelerate' path depends on rhythm and predictability. It relies on quarterly targets, compliance routines and clear accountabilities. The 'transform' path depends on exploration. It relies on short experiments, rough prototypes and rapid learning. Trying to judge both with the same KPIs is a huge mistake.

Governance must separate cadence, but not attention. Your board and executive should review two dashboards side by side. One tracks the performance of the core business innovation work. The other tracks the learning velocity of the transformation initiatives. These should be reviewed together to maintain alignment, but never through the same scorecard.

Your 'core' business dashboard measures efficiency, reliability and margin, while your 'next' business dashboard measures validated progress, customer signal and learning speed. The point is not balance but coherence. Everyone sees the whole system, but no-one expects improvement and invention to behave alike. That distinction is what makes dual transformation stable rather than chaotic.

Use gains from faster trains to fuel the aircraft before the money drops away

AI delivers savings quickly. Cycle times shrink, error rates fall and workflows compress. These productivity gains are usually absorbed into next year's budget and lost. Once that happens, it becomes increasingly harder to fund new transformation work – especially given its long payback periods.

Dual transformation works only when savings from the core business are redirected into transformation initiatives for the next business. Every improvement on the rails extends runway for the aircraft. Every insight from the aircraft reveals new opportunities to modernise the rails. This loop creates a self-funding system, shifting the organisation from annual budgeting to continuous reinvestment. Waiting for future cycles guarantees the fuel will evaporate.

This discipline is often the hardest shift for leaders. It requires protecting money that finance would normally capture, and a willingness to invest in work that may not pay off quickly. But without this loop, your transformation programs will be starved of capital.

Move talent with intent, not convenience

Left alone, the best people gather in the existing business, because this is where status and career hierarchy live. It is where certainty resides. It is where performance is easiest to measure. But the transformation program needs some of these people. It needs their judgement, pattern recognition and credibility.

You must rotate talent in your organisation deliberately. Let high performers spend time in 'transform' discovery work. Let product leads and operations managers contribute to experiments at the edge. Expose people from the reinvention program to the core business so they understand scale, reliability and consequence. The point is not cross-training. It is perspective.

When people experience both paths, they stop treating them as competing priorities. The core business improvement teams understand the new business ambition. The invention teams respect the discipline of the legacy business. Curiosity circulates and empathy grows. The organisation becomes fluent in both.

Install a control tower to choreograph two speeds

These programs do not stay aligned on their own. Instead, someone must manage the tension. Someone must decide when to move resources, when to share learning and when to keep distance. Someone must prevent the railway from starving the airline of funding.

The control tower your organisation installs to manage these tensions is usually a small cross-functional group led by the CEO or chief strategy officer. This group should meet every quarter to monitor the rhythm of improvement and the pace of invention. They can assess whether the day-to day innovation work is stable and whether the new-growth work has enough runway. They can decide which experiments progress, which pause and which retire. They can remove political friction before it hardens and maintain tension at the right level.

Without this structure, organisations oscillate. They over-invest in the new work too early. They protect the incumbent model for too long. They shift direction every budget cycle. The control tower provides a steady metronome for running two speeds at once.

When these five shifts come together, your organisation can stop mistaking activity for progress. The core becomes a steady engine of capability, cash and trust. The transform stream becomes a disciplined explorer rather than a speculative distraction. Both contribute to a shared future. Momentum replaces noise and direction replaces drift.

Dual transformation becomes a practice rather than an aspiration. It becomes the way your organisation strengthens what already works while building what comes next.

Playbook: The transformation compass

Each of the following five questions is a pressure test. Together they reveal whether you are building faster trains, designing aircraft or attempting both without the structure to support it. Ask yourself:

1. **What is the true level of disruption in our industry?** Is your platform warming or is it burning? Look at customer behaviour, margin pressure and competitor capability (and flip back to chapter 4 if you need more of a refresher). Improvement is enough when the fundamentals still hold. Transformation is required when your business model cannot deliver what the market now expects.

2. **Are we investing more in efficiency than adaptability?** The optimise discipline delivers productivity and cost savings. Accelerate delivers revenue and customer uplift. But if all the investment sits in improving the core business, you may be blindsided if the industry is being disrupted by AI. Dial in levels of efficiency and adaptability as needed.
3. **Do we have one transformation or two?** Faster trains are a single transformation, and this is most relevant for organisations not facing significant disruption. Dual transformation is used when you need to build the 'next' while maintaining the 'core'. Be explicit. If the work of invention is buried inside improvement, it will suffocate. If improvement is ignored in the rush to invent, the core will feel the pain of distraction.
4. **Which path fits our appetite for disruptive transformation: build, buy or partner?** This is a strategic choice, not an opportunistic one. Building gives control. Buying trades money for time. Partnering trades control for speed. Your decision shapes the culture, timeline and risk profile.
5. **How are we measuring learning speed, not just output?** Legacy businesses reward performance. Transformation programs require validated learning. If your scorecards optimise output alone, you will never make the transition to the new. Learning velocity is the hidden indicator that reveals whether the new business is viable.

Provocation: Final approach

Every generation of leaders faces its own disruptive moment. For the industrialists, it was electricity. For the digital pioneers, it was the internet. For us, it is AI.

You can keep improving what you already do. You can tighten processes, optimise cost, and celebrate a business that runs smoothly and predictably. The world will praise your efficiency right up until it chooses a different way of getting the same outcome. Operational excellence is impressive, but it is only valuable while customers still value what it delivers.

Incremental improvement feels safe. Invention can feel reckless. Most organisations over-invest in the former and hesitate on the latter. They tell themselves the gap will close. They wait for clarity. They wait for data. They wait for alignment. Meanwhile, others are building entirely new ways to deliver value.

AI exposes every assumption your core business was built on. It compresses timelines, accelerates rivals and rewrites expectations you once thought immovable. By the time the disruption is visible, your customers may have already moved on.

You have an advantage. As an incumbent player, your organisation already holds the customer relationships and the trust they represent. Most challengers would trade anything for that head start. The question is whether you use it.

You can build faster trains. You can build aircraft. You can choose both if disruption demands it. But you cannot wait. Not now.

So here is the final decision. Do you keep extending the track? Or do you start building the vehicle that carries you beyond it?

What's next

The real constraint is no longer imagination but architecture. You can understand where the future is headed and pursue parallel transformations, yet still stall if the organisation is built for a slower, more sequential world. Strategy can now operate at machine speed. Structure often cannot.

The next chapter shifts the focus from direction to design. From deciding which future to pursue, to examining whether your operating model, decision rights and talent systems are capable of supporting it. AI does not just change what work is done. It changes how work flows, who decides, and how quickly the organisation can learn and act.

The question is no longer simply what you want to become. It is whether your organisation is built to handle intelligence at scale.

CHAPTER 9

Built for intelligence

One of the underrated perks of consulting is the sheer variety of human behaviour you get to witness in its natural habitat. (I mean that in the nicest possible way.)

I can walk into one organisation and it feels like a well-run cockpit. I can identify clear roles, clean decisions and fast feedback. Everyone knows what matters and why. I leave thinking, *Right, this is what 'high performing' actually looks like when it is not just a slide.* Then I can walk into another organisation and it is more like a museum – just the exhibits are still operational.

Seeing these differences is the bit I love. And, if I am honest, it is also the bit that keeps me sane. I get bored. I get frustrated. And a special comfort comes in knowing that, unlike most employees, I can eventually leave the building. Consultants can absolutely overstay their welcome. (Trust me, I have been one who has. You start out as a guest and, before you know it, you are basically an oddly dressed piece of furniture.)

Working across lots of clients also means I can build pattern recognition quickly. My team and I have had the privilege of working alongside some genuinely exceptional CEOs and leadership teams. These are people who run crisp operations with serious talent. They are decisive without being reckless. They move fast without being chaotic. They make the hard call, and then move on. In those environments, technology becomes a lever, amplifying what is already true.

And then, occasionally, I see something that makes me wonder if I have accidentally time travelled. I'm not going to name names (obviously; I enjoy being invited back), but I have witnessed some mind-boggling practices. I have sat with leaders, for example, who print their emails every morning – not 'important ones'; all of them. I've seen a full inbox, fresh from the server, transformed into a neat stack of paper like a daily news bulletin from 1997. They have then highlighted things and circled sentences. They've written 'pls action' in the margin. And then they've handed them to someone who scanned the annotated pages so they could be forwarded back to the very people who originally sent the email. It was a complete loop of modern communication, carefully re-routed through a printer.

I have also watched contracts drafted digitally, printed so someone can sign them with a pen, and then scanned back into the system so they can be emailed as a PDF. Bonus points when the signature is required 'for audit purposes', and even better when the audit trail turns out to be a forwarded email chain living in someone's Sent folder, right next to a reminder about a dentist appointment.

And then there is the spreadsheet. You know the one: the *critical process* spreadsheet. It's the spreadsheet that runs a major part of the business and owned by one person – who is always on leave at exactly the wrong time. It has tabs called FINAL, FINAL2, FINAL_REALLY_FINAL, and a hidden macro nobody understands but everyone fears touching. It is both a tool and a hostage situation. The organisation does not run on data. It runs on whether that one person is online.

To be clear, these things are funny. We have chuckled behind closed doors. Sometimes, we have chuckled in front of open doors, and then quickly pretended it was a cough. But the bigger point is not the comedy. It is the signal.

These practices did not appear because people were foolish. They appeared because, at some point, they were sensible. Printing emails made sense when trust lived on paper. Wet signatures made sense when risk was managed through physical artefacts. The spreadsheet made sense when systems were expensive and speed was not the constraint.

The problem is that the environment has changed and the organisation has not.

AI is now capable of generating insight faster than most teams can schedule the meeting to discuss it. Information no longer sits neatly at the top of a hierarchy waiting to be handed down. It arrives everywhere, constantly. Patterns surface before humans know what to ask. Decisions need to move with the tempo of the world, not the tempo of the calendar.

And that is the paradox many leaders are now trapped inside. The tools have surged ahead, but the organisation is still catching up. **The technology is not the hard part anymore. The hard part is the operating model wrapped around it** – including the structure, decision rights, rhythm and trust.

The problem is the way humans collect inside companies to turn information into action.

Intelligence has entered the system, but the system itself is not yet intelligent.

Machine-speed tools and human-speed organisations

Organisations today face a simple reality: the tools have surged ahead, but the teams and structures have not. The technology is moving fast, yet organisations are still built for a slower, more predictable world. This creates a tension in leadership conversations. Everyone can feel the pressure building, but the organisation still responds with reflexes shaped by an earlier era.

AI can now scan markets, write code, predict demand and even summarise board papers. It can generate insights before most teams have finished loading the spreadsheet. Yet most organisations still make decisions as if it were 1995. They rely on meetings, hand-offs and layers of approval that once kept the business safe but now only slow it down. They're flooded with machine-speed data, but their structures move at a walking pace. The gap between what a business knows and what it can actually do keeps growing, stretching leadership attention thinner every year.

Inside many firms, intelligence is abundant but trapped. Data flows through a dozen dashboards, yet few people have permission or the capability to act on it. Automation accelerates production, but sign-offs stall delivery. Pilots pop up everywhere, but none of them scale, and after the third steering committee enthusiasm begins to fade. The organisation becomes a paradox of progress: technically advanced but operationally paralysed. Leaders talk about transformation, yet the machinery beneath them still prefers stability to movement.

The real problem isn't the technology. It's the way we've built around it. We have tried to graft intelligent tools onto unintelligent structures. We have tried to run machine-speed systems through management habits designed for slower, calmer times. The result is predictable. The organisation feels smarter on the surface, but heavier at the core.

We've spent years digitising our tools, but we haven't redesigned the organism that uses them. We wired our companies for efficiency, but the real edge now is agility: the ability to sense, decide and move faster than competitors, customers or even change itself. Efficiency made sense when the world was steady. Now it only makes companies brittle.

AI has made this contradiction impossible to ignore. It exposes the distance between awareness and action. It reveals how quickly your organisation learns and how slowly it responds. It forces you as a leader to confront a simple truth you can no longer avoid: intelligence has entered the system, but the system itself isn't intelligent.

Building the system that learns

In this chapter, I introduce the Intelligent Operating Model: a blueprint for rebuilding how your organisation thinks and works in the age of AI. Your focus shouldn't be on adding more tools or spinning up a new set of pilots. It should be on designing the organisational architecture so intelligence can flow, rather than collecting point solutions that never speak to one another. This approach offers a way for human direction and machine capability to reinforce each other rather than fight for control, authority, or ownership of decisions.

The model rests on two interdependent systems. The first, the intelligence core, is where human intent lives. Strategy, trust, empathy and governance sit here. This is the part of the organisation that defines what matters, what is protected and what the business is willing to automate. It ensures that every AI decision begins with purpose and ends with accountability. The second system, the AI operating spine, is the technical and procedural backbone that makes intelligence scalable. It includes the shared data, models, evaluation tools and assurance services that keep automation consistent, compliant and observable. When these two systems work together, they form a continuous learning loop. The core sets direction. The spine delivers and monitors execution. The feedback between them refines both.

Your goal isn't to make your organisation more digital but more responsive. Old hierarchies were built for stability. AI asks for adaptability. The Intelligent Operating Model gives you a way to have both as a leader: speed without chaos, autonomy without risk, and innovation without losing the human pulse of judgement and empathy. It allows your organisation to move at the tempo of its own intelligence rather than the tempo of its inherited structure.

What follows is a framework for finding that balance, and for wiring your organisation so its strategy, structure and culture can learn as quickly as the technology that now drives them.

Why now: When structure becomes the bottleneck

Most organisations weren't designed for intelligent work. They were designed for predictable work. Their architecture reflects a world where the future behaved like the past, where variance signalled risk and where slowing decisions down was a responsible act. Layers of management were built to control uncertainty, not accelerate learning. Information now travels faster than decisions. Insight is produced at machine speed, while the structures interpreting it still move at human speed.

This gap between knowing and acting is now the new competitive fault line. Every company faces the same challenge: the faster AI learns, the slower the old hierarchy seems. Leaders feel the lag long before they can explain it. Something that once protected performance now inhibits it.

Three structural forces make the old model untenable:

- **Cognitive distribution:** Expertise has escaped the org chart and no longer sits neatly within departments or job titles. It spans systems, data, models, agents and external contributors. Knowledge work is becoming networked work. Without architecture that connects human judgement to machine intelligence, organisations end up running on partial sight. They become data rich but insight poor, with intelligence scattered across tools instead of concentrated in decisions.
- **Trust fragility:** As decisions migrate into algorithms, trust becomes the scarcest organisational resource. Employees need confidence that automation won't hollow out their judgement or accelerate experience scarcity.

Customers need confidence that AI-driven outcomes are fair, explainable and accountable. Boards need confidence that risk and reliability have not been outsourced to a black box. Without trust, speed becomes recklessness, automation becomes noise and intelligent tools become liabilities rather than levers of advantage.

- **Time compression:** Decision cycles that once spanned quarters now unfold in hours. Markets reprice, customers shift and models retrain overnight. The rhythm of work has accelerated, but the rhythm of management hasn't.

Strategy still happens annually. Budgets still move in slow tranches. Priorities wait for meetings scheduled weeks in advance. Leadership cadence no longer matches the cadence of change, and every delay compounds the cost of inaction.

Agility, not efficiency, is now the real test of resilience. Efficiency optimises for the known. Agility adapts to the unknown. The problem isn't that companies can't move faster. It's that their systems hold them back.

The Intelligent Operating Model solves this by aligning structure with speed, reconnecting intent with information, and turning your organisation into a learning organism that moves in step with its own intelligence. It closes the gap between awareness and action, giving you an organisation that can sense, decide and adjust with the same tempo as the technology it now depends on.

The framework: The Intelligent Operating Model

If AI has changed the dynamics of business, the Intelligent Operating Model changes its anatomy. It reconfigures how intelligence moves, how decisions are made and how your organisation learns. It trades static hierarchy for dynamic connection, shifting the enterprise from a structure that pushes information upward to one that lets intelligence move in every direction at once. It turns your organisation into something closer to a living system, one that adjusts to pressure, responds to feedback and senses the world around it with far greater accuracy.

Most organisations still behave as if knowledge sits at the top and action sits at the bottom. AI has broken that logic. Information now originates everywhere. Patterns are detected by systems before humans know where to look. Insights arrive before meetings begin. The Intelligent Operating Model is the response to this new reality. It is not a technical blueprint but an organisational one. It ensures your business can absorb intelligence without slowing it, blocking it or allowing it to pool in corners of the hierarchy where nobody can act on it.

Intelligent Operating Model

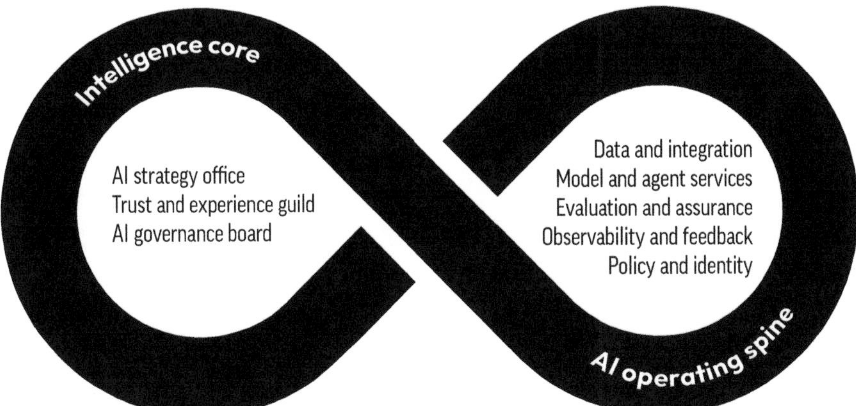

As mentioned, the model has two interdependent systems: the intelligence core and the AI operating spine. Together, they form a closed loop between human intent and machine intelligence, shown in the previous figure. One provides meaning while the other provides momentum. And the feedback junction between them ensures that both keep learning as the organisation accelerates.

This section maps the full anatomy of that system: what it contains, how it functions and how it transforms the organisation into one that can think, adapt and move at the same tempo as its own intelligence.

The intelligence core: The human system of meaning

Every intelligent organisation begins with human clarity. Purpose, values and boundaries set the conditions in which AI can operate. The intelligence core within the Intelligent Operating Model holds this clarity. It is the place where strategic direction, trust and governance live. If the core is weak, AI becomes disconnected and chaotic. If the core is strong, AI becomes a force multiplier for organisational intent.

The intelligence core has three primary functions.

The AI strategy office: Direction and focus

At the centre of the core sits the AI strategy office, providing the organisation's sense of direction. Its role is to translate ambition into focus. It clarifies where AI creates advantage, which problems matter most and what pace the enterprise can sustain without breaking its own foundations. It is the mechanism for connecting corporate strategy to AI strategy, and is the primary lever through which the CEO and senior executives influence AI outcomes.

The strategy office is not a project management office with a new coat of paint. It is a decision engine. It sequences initiatives so teams do not drown in competing priorities. It aligns resources so investment follows intent rather than novelty. It forces trade-offs, even when they are uncomfortable. It keeps attention fixed on your North Star (refer to chapter 5) and ensures that every initiative fits within the guardrails defined by the automation envelope (chapter 3).

When the strategy office is missing, signs appear quickly. The organisation moves but without orientation. Teams experiment without coordination. Pilots accumulate but do not compound. The business learns but cannot scale what it learns. Over time, the gap between activity and progress widens.

The strategy office closes that gap. It turns direction into discipline and ensures the organisation knows not only where it is going, but also why it is going there.

The trust and experience guild: The human pulse

Alongside the strategy office sits the trust and experience guild. This function protects the organisation's human equilibrium. It exists because efficiency is easy to count while experience is easy to lose. And when experience degrades, judgement weakens with it.

The guild ensures that automation does not hollow out capability. It watches for erosion in the formative work that develops judgement. It tracks indicators such as employee confidence, customer trust and the quality of decision-making within critical workflows. It monitors where AI enhances human contribution and where it begins to replace the very experiences people need to stay competent.

The guild seems soft until it is missing. Then the signals appear. Teams become dependent on the tools they are meant to supervise. Juniors lose the practice that builds their judgement. Customers feel the absence of empathy. Leaders begin to sense fragility in places where resilience used to live.

The guild stops this drift. It is not cultural decoration but structural risk management. It ensures that the craft of the professions is appropriately safeguarded. When empathy and trust collapses, automation collapses with it. When experience thins, capability thins with it. The guild creates balance, ensuring your organisation can accelerate without destabilising itself.

The AI governance board: Boundaries and assurance

The final function within the core is the AI governance board. It defines the organisation's boundaries, determining where AI can act and where it must not. It establishes escalation pathways, clarifies responsibilities and ensures risks are understood rather than discovered too late.

Governance often carries a reputation for slowing things down. In intelligent organisations, it does the opposite. When teams know the rules, they act faster. When the limits are explicit, experimentation becomes safer. When risk is monitored, scale becomes possible.

The governance board gives your organisation moral and operational clarity. It ensures that speed never outruns accountability and that automation never escapes its intended purpose. With clear boundaries, intelligent systems become predictable partners rather than unpredictable liabilities.

Together, these three functions form the human heartbeat of the organisation. The core gives meaning to intelligence. It ensures your organisation knows what it stands for, how it learns and what it will never compromise.

The AI operating spine: The machine system of intelligence

Where the core provides meaning, the spine provides momentum. It is the infrastructure that turns intelligence into action. It ensures that insights move quickly, safely and reliably to the teams who need them. It is the difference between an organisation that experiments and an organisation that compounds.

The spine consists of five layers that build on each other to create a complete system.

Data and integration layer: Clean flow

At the base of the spine is the data and integration layer. It ensures that information flows across the organisation rather than sitting in silos. It transforms scattered pockets of intelligence into a unified nervous system.

When this layer is weak, AI becomes brittle; models break and insights degrade. People stop trusting the systems meant to help them. Clean flow from this layer is not optional. It is the foundation on which everything else depends.

Model and agent services layer: Shared capability

Above the plumbing sits the model and agent services layer. This provides shared access to the organisation's AI capabilities. It includes foundation models, fine-tuning pipelines, reusable agents and orchestration tools.

This layer prevents duplication. Without it, teams rebuild the same solution repeatedly. With it, innovation compounds. Your organisation learns faster because every capability becomes reusable rather than disposable.

Evaluation and assurance layer: Confidence and control

The evaluation and assurance layer keeps automation honest. It tests models for bias, drift and reliability. It ensures systems behave in line with expectations and reveals hidden risks before they turn into operational failures.

Confidence is not a feeling but a function. This layer delivers it.

Observability and feedback layer: Closed loops

The observability and feedback layer monitors usage in the real world. It flags anomalies, records drift, highlights friction and exposes where AI behaves differently from what leadership expects.

This layer is the connective tissue between the spine and the core of the Intelligent Operating Model. It feeds insights back into leadership cycles, shortening the time between discovery and decision, and turning each interaction into a learning event.

Policy and identity layer: Traceability and accountability

At the top of the spine sits the policy and identity layer. It authenticates users, authorises actions and keeps decisions traceable. It ensures accountability remains visible even as automation increases.

This layer protects the organisation when things go well and when they do not. It provides the confidence you need as a leader to scale without losing control.

The feedback junction: Where learning lives

Between the core and the spine lies the feedback junction. This is where human purpose meets machine precision. Data flows upward. Direction flows downward. Action becomes insight. Insight becomes action. This loop turns the organisation into a learning system rather than a controlled one.

When the junction is weak, intelligence leaks. Patterns stay unrecognised and lessons remain local instead of becoming organisational. But when the junction is strong, your organisation begins to feel alive. It senses opportunity, adjusts behaviour and becomes capable of learning from itself.

This junction is the heart of the Intelligent Operating Model. It ensures your organisation moves at the speed of its own intelligence rather than the speed of its old hierarchy.

Application: Executing the transformation

Once your AI strategy is clear, the real work becomes architectural. The goal is not to bolt AI onto old structures, but to rebuild how the organisation learns. Most transformations stall because leaders treat AI as a technology rollout rather than a redesign of rhythm, roles and relationships. They focus on tools long before they examine incentives. They automate tasks long before they address decision rights. They ask teams to work faster inside systems designed to work slowly. The Intelligent Operating Model reframes transformation as a shift in how the enterprise senses, decides and adapts.

Aligning the system around a shared centre of gravity

The starting point is alignment. Strategy, trust and governance must evolve together rather than in sequence. When any one of them races ahead, the organisation loses its footing. The AI strategy office sets the tempo by narrowing priorities and converting broad ambition into practical focus. The governance board anchors that focus by defining the boundaries that make acceleration safe rather than reckless. The trust and experience guild protects the human foundations that keep judgement strong as automation expands. Each reinforces the others. When all three speak the same language, momentum becomes deliberate rather than frantic. When they diverge, transformation becomes theatre.

This alignment depends on a new relationship with feedback. Most organisations still operate with reporting rhythms built for a world that moved more slowly. Data travels upwards. Interpretation happens in meetings. Insight becomes stale before anyone has acted on it. The operating spine is intended to invert this pattern by making telemetry (the automated process of collecting and transmitting data from remote sources) a living input to leadership rather than a retrospective artefact. Performance signals flow continuously. Risk indicators surface early. Data about model behaviour becomes part of ordinary decision-making rather than an annual audit. Quarterly intelligence reviews replace annual retrospectives because the business cannot afford to wait a year to notice what is changing. The aim is not to create an avalanche of analytics but to shrink the distance between observation and action.

When alignment and feedback reinforce each other, your organisation begins to develop a shared centre of gravity.

Decisions become more consistent, intent becomes clearer and the system moves as one rather than in fragments.

Shifting how management works

As the feedback system matures, management itself begins to shift. When AI handles coordination, monitoring and reporting, the work of managing moves away from supervision and towards sense-making. Managers no longer add value by moving information. They add value by interpreting context and clarifying intent. They become translators between organisational purpose and on-the-ground complexity. This requires different decision rights. Authority needs to sit closer to the information rather than higher in the hierarchy. Boundaries become more important than approvals. Judgement becomes a distributed capability rather than a periodic escalation.

This shift also exposes the need for a new operational tempo. Traditional programs rely on fixed phases and linear plans. AI refuses to cooperate with that logic and instead evolves constantly. It exposes new behaviours and new risks as it is used. Projects designed a year earlier no longer match the reality of today. Cadence solves this problem. Using 90-day operating cycles creates a tempo where strategy, delivery, trust indicators and governance checkpoints travel together. Your whole organisation breathes in the same rhythm. Learning becomes continuous rather than episodic. Adjustments become routine rather than dramatic. Cadence turns intelligent work into a habit rather than a special initiative.

When your management team moves from supervision to interpretation, and when tempo shifts from annual planning to rolling cycles, your organisation can stop waiting for alignment and start producing it through its own rhythm.

Embedding new behaviours into the system

Structural change is necessary, but behavioural change is mandatory. People act inside the constraints and affordances of the system that surrounds them. If roles are unclear, decisions slow. If incentives reward old behaviours, new workflows stall. If trust signals are invisible, people retreat. The Intelligent Operating Model works because it aligns architecture with behaviour. It makes it easier to act in ways that compound intelligence and harder to act in ways that fragment it. Culture begins to change because the system gives it no choice.

The pace of change must also be sequenced. Intelligent organisations do not attempt to rebuild themselves in one decisive sweep. They iterate and strengthen foundations before layering on complexity. They install new decision rhythms before removing legacy ones. They adjust governance before releasing autonomy. These shifts accumulate quietly. Teams feel them through reduced friction, cleaner decisions, faster feedback and clearer priorities. The organisation becomes more responsive not through grand announcements, but through a series of small, increasingly reliable improvements.

Throughout this process, purpose functions as the anchor. AI can accelerate anything and so, without grounding, it can accelerate confusion. Without boundaries, it accelerates risk. Without human judgement, it accelerates error. The Intelligent Operating Model ensures purpose sits at the centre of the system. The intelligence core holds meaning. The operating spine carries intelligence. The feedback junction connects the two. That connection ensures acceleration reinforces the organisation's identity rather than eroding it.

When these shifts take hold, AI stops being a project and becomes part of how the company thinks. Leadership regains visibility while teams regain agency and decisions become cleaner. The rhythm of the organisation begins to match the rhythm of the world around it, and the distance between knowing and doing narrows. Strategy and execution stop behaving like separate domains. Transformation stops feeling like a program and starts feeling like a new operating reality.

This is when the system begins to work for you rather than against you. Intelligent work becomes the default, not the aspiration. Your organisation becomes capable of moving at the speed of its own insight.

Playbook: Turning design into movement

The Intelligent Operating Model only works when it becomes lived practice rather than architectural intent. These principles translate structure into motion:

1. **Wire direction and discipline together:** AI strategy and governance must operate as a single system. Treat the AI strategy office and the governance board as complementary forces. One sets ambition while the other sets limits. When they work in isolation, confusion spreads. When they work in tension, clarity grows.
2. **Make feedback the management system:** Swap static reporting for live telemetry. Assurance data,

drift signals and usage patterns should shape everyday decisions. The faster the feedback, the fewer the surprises. Leaders cannot wait for annual reviews to discover whether intelligence is compounding or leaking.

3. **Redefine management as sense-making:** Managers should stop chasing updates and start interpreting meaning. Their job is to turn information into clarity. They curate context, highlight risk and connect action to intent. This is how judgement scales without slowing the organisation.
4. **Treat trust as infrastructure:** The trust and experience guild safeguards the human elements that keep the system resilient. Empathy and trust are not cultural decoration but operational stability. Measure them with the same discipline used for throughput and performance.
5. **Institutionalise rhythm:** Replace transformation programs with rolling 90-day cycles. Rhythm aligns strategy, delivery and governance. It keeps your organisation learning in public and moving at the speed of its own intelligence.

The provocation: Intelligence starts with design

Most organisations are not held back by technology. They are held back by the architecture that surrounds it. AI moves at the speed of learning and feedback. Most companies move at the speed of approval. That gap is now the defining weakness, along with being the easiest to ignore.

Many leadership teams still run 20th-century systems with 21st-century tools. They automate tasks but protect rituals. They install AI agents but keep the same meetings. They celebrate pilots while their operating model continues to slow every important decision. Nothing breaks quickly. It just drifts, and then it snaps.

The Intelligent Operating Model shows how intelligence really moves through your organisation. It reveals who learns, who delays and who decides. It exposes the gap between what leaders claim to value and what the system actually rewards.

That is why this work feels personal. You are not redesigning a structure but rewiring reflexes. You are teaching the enterprise to sense and respond rather than wait and justify. You are choosing whether intelligence flows or fragments.

The uncomfortable part is simple. **AI does not make an organisation intelligent. It only reveals whether it already is.** It amplifies clarity and confusion, and accelerates whatever is already true.

So ask the questions that matter:

- If your organisation could think for itself, what would it say?
- Would it ask to move faster?
- Would it ask for fewer gates?
- Would it ask for trust?
- Or would it quietly admit that the system you built cannot keep up with the intelligence you now depend on?

Your answer is not technical. It is architectural.

CONCLUSION

After expertise

The inspiration for this book came from a very funny place. It started, as many bad ideas these days do, with me discovering yet another AI tool and announcing it to the team like I had personally invented electricity. I am fairly notorious at Humanly Agile for being a bit of a geek. I love to tinker. I love to prod buttons I should not prod. And I love the moment something moves from 'interesting' to 'useful'.

Josh, one of my senior team members, has developed a specific look for these moments. It is not quite an eye roll and more like a controlled facial screensaver, as if his operating system is trying to protect itself from new information. When I say, 'I've found something incredible', Josh hears, 'I've found something that will consume three weeks of our lives and end in disappointment'.

He is not always wrong.

Over the past few years, we have done what we tell our clients to do. We have embedded AI deeply inside our business, not as a side project but as a way of working. We have built a small cast of AI agents and given them real jobs. They are AI-powered digital co-workers that can take a brief, decide the next steps and complete tasks. Hermione handles client research. Rupert helps us with recruiting. Beatrice scopes and designs agents. Jess runs executive-level voice interviews inside our AI strategy work. They are not toys. They are part of the team.

We have also had a ridiculous amount of fun implementing them and watching them work. Something is strangely satisfying about watching an agent do in minutes what used to take someone a morning, without the sighing, the copying and pasting, or the quiet resentment. The impacts have also been real. Our clients have loved seeing AI in action. And, if I am honest, I have loved it because it scratches a deep itch in me – the itch that says, 'Surely we can do this better'.

But every story needs a villain, and ours came in the form of two white whales.

The first was an agent that could reliably produce client-facing PowerPoint decks. We didn't want rough drafts or internal working slides. We wanted the actual thing we ship; the kind of deck that represents our judgement, our taste and our reputation.

The second was 'Emily', our prototype AI executive assistant. (The name is not subtle. My guilty pleasure is rewatching *The Devil Wears Prada* – if you know, you know.) I wanted an EA with immaculate competence, light menace and a complete intolerance for my ability to create chaos in my own calendar.

Josh calls these 'the whales' because, like all white whales, they have a habit of surfacing just long enough to remind you they exist, and then disappearing again, leaving you cold, wet and questioning your life choices.

We could get the PowerPoint agent to produce slides that looked … fine. It could follow templates, write headlines and even build a reasonable storyline if you squinted and lowered your expectations. But that was the problem.

Consulting decks are not won on 'reasonable'. They are won on the nuance that comes from having sat in too many rooms, listened to too many executives, watched too many initiatives fail for boring reasons, and learned to anticipate what the audience is going to misunderstand before they misunderstand it.

A good slide is not a rectangle with words. It is a series of decisions. It is deciding what to include, what to cut, what to name and what to imply. Deciding where to be blunt, and where to be kind. When to push, when to protect the relationship, and when to avoid cleverness and just tell the truth.

We found that we could teach AI the expertise. We could show it the formats, frameworks and 'how to build a deck' mechanics. But we could not easily transfer the experience. Over 30 years of professional scar tissue does not come in a PDF.

The failure was even more obvious with Emily. On the surface, executive assistance looks like the perfect automation candidate. The job is all about your calendar, email, scheduling, briefings, follow-ups and reminders. You think it's just a lot of structured work, repeatable patterns, endless admin and a strong need for speed. And then you meet a great EA.

I am extremely lucky to be supported by Pamela, the best EA I have ever worked with. She is a weapon. This is not her first rodeo, and I am very much not her first difficult executive.

Pamela does not just manage tasks. She manages judgement.

She is constantly making calls that do not look like calls until you understand what is at stake. She makes the call, for example, on which meeting matters more when two clash, and which client needs a response in the next hour and which one can wait until tomorrow without consequence. She decides which invitation is genuinely important and which one is professional theatre, as well as which 'quick catch-up' is actually going to become a negotiation, and which one is just someone being nervous and needing reassurance.

She also manages emotion, and mostly mine.

She calibrates tone and reads context. She knows when I am energised, when I am distracted, and when I am about to say yes to something stupid because I am in a good mood and someone used the word 'exciting'.

A great EA is not a calendar manager but a trust system.

You only appreciate how much empathy and relationship work sits inside that role when you try to automate it. An AI agent can schedule, summarise and draft. But it cannot feel the weight of a relationship, sense the political temperature in a thread, or notice that a one-line reply will be read as disrespect even if it is technically correct. It cannot do any of these tasks reliably, safely or at the standard you would bet your day on.

Realising this with our two 'white whales' was the moment the core idea of this book emerged – not from theory but from friction.

We could automate expertise. We could compress it, scale it, package it and hand it around the organisation like it was a commodity. But the real value, the stuff that made outcomes better rather than merely faster, lived somewhere else. It lived in experience, judgement under uncertainty, consequence-bearing decisions, and the patterns you only recognise after you have made a few mistakes in public. It lived in emotion and empathy, trust earned over time, relationships protected in small moments and the human legitimacy that makes change stick.

Those two white whales did us a favour. They exposed the boundary between what machines can do and what organisations still need humans to be. And once we saw it, we could not unsee it.

So we did what we always do when something refuses to behave in a neat way. We took it on the road. We tested the thinking with about ten of our biggest clients during AI strategy engagements. We considered different industries, different risk postures and different cultures, and we noticed the same pattern. The same questions surfaced again and again, sometimes spoken, often not:

- Where do we automate without hollowing out capability?
- Where do we augment so people become better, not just faster?
- How do we protect the experiences that create judgement, especially when automation makes those experiences optional?
- How do we maintain empathy and trust when machines start doing work that used to signal competence?

Along the way, I gave keynotes, board briefings and workshops. I watched leaders nod at the exciting parts, and then pause at the uncomfortable bits. Someone fell asleep once (long story – don't ask). I kept refining the language until it matched what was actually happening in organisations, not what we wished was happening.

The models in this book are not perfect, and they are not meant to be. Perfection is a luxury item in a world that is moving this quickly. But they are stress tested.

They have been shaped by real constraints, real politics, real trade-offs and real people trying to do good work while the ground shifts under them. They were built in the imperfect world, which is the only world you get to lead in.

If you take one thing from this book, take this: AI will make you faster at expertise, but it will not make you wiser. That part is still on you.

Your job now is not to fight the machines, or worship them or pretend nothing has changed. Your job is to design work so that automation strengthens your organisation rather than thinning it out. You need to set boundaries before you scale, protect minimum viable experience before it disappears, and treat trust as infrastructure, not decoration. And, occasionally, you need to notice what your own white whales are trying to teach you.

Josh still rolls his eyes when I announce the latest tool. Pamela still saves me from myself. The agents still do a startling amount of work. The difference now is that we know what we are optimising for. We're not looking for more output but better judgement, stronger trust and a more human edge. That is what will compound.

The work starts now. Good luck

Getting in touch

If you made it this far, thank you. Seriously. Writing a book is a strange, solitary thing. Reading one all the way through is an act of quiet generosity – and one I appreciate.

If this book sparked ideas, questions, arguments or the uncomfortable feeling that something probably needs to change, I would genuinely love to hear from you. The easiest place to find me is LinkedIn. I am fairly active there, and it is where most good conversations seem to start these days.

I work with a small number of organisations each year on AI strategy and transformation programs. We don't focus on pilots for the sake of pilots or on technology theatre, but on the hard work of deciding what to automate, what to augment, what to protect and how to build capability that lasts. If that is something you are grappling with, feel free to get in touch.

I am also available for keynotes, leadership offsites and workshops where the goal is not hype but clarity. I enjoy rooms where people are thinking seriously about the future of work and are prepared to challenge their own assumptions.

You can reach me via:

- www.humanlyagile.com
- info@humanlyagile.com

Or simply scan the QR code.

Thanks again for reading. And, if nothing else, I hope this book helped you ask better questions. That is usually where the real work begins.

To those who made it happen

First and always, my thanks go to my family. **Sam**, **Phoebe**, **Harrison** and **Imogen**, **Felix** and **Tilly**. You have supported me through the full roller-coaster of ideas, deadlines and distracted conversations, put up with my bullshit, and never hesitated to offer the highest form of praise available in our household – that the work was 'not horrific'. You have lived with this book long before anyone else had to read it. I am endlessly grateful for your patience and perspective.

Next, my absolute partner in crime, **Joshua Clarkson**. Josh has worked alongside me every step of the way, helping to develop these ideas and, more importantly, pressure-testing them in the real world with our clients at Humanly Agile. He has also shown saint-like tolerance for the never-ending train of AI tools I keep introducing with great enthusiasm and limited warning. This book would not exist without your partnership, judgement and humour.

Melissa Cupples deserves special mention. My best friend and now Head of Intelligent Product and AI at Humanly Agile,

Melissa has an uncanny ability to challenge my thinking while simultaneously expanding it. She pushes ideas further and sharpens the edges, and then calmly goes off and teaches people how to build AI agents at scale. Rockstar is not an overstatement; however, the responses to text messages have only marginally improved since the last book.

It goes without saying that my rock remains my superhuman EA, **Pamela Ellis**. Pamela deals with my chaos daily, keeps the wheels on when they should absolutely have fallen off, and performs feats of coordination that no AI agent could come close to replicating. I cannot thank you enough and I have no intention of ever trying to replace you with software.

To the wider **Humanly Agile** team and associates, including **Karen**, **Raul** and the broader crew, thank you for tolerating my daily madness and my serious lack of availability while this book was being written. Your professionalism, patience and good humour made it possible for me to disappear into writing mode without the business imploding. That is no small achievement.

Two people deserve very specific thanks. **Ian McCall** is still, without question, the strategy mind I call when I have dug myself into a deep conceptual hole. Much of the foundational AI strategy thinking that informed this book was shaped by Ian calmly explaining why my initial ideas were mad, and then patiently guiding me towards something far more elegant. That combination of honesty and generosity is rare.

Ashan Ponnusamy also needs recognition. An exceptional friend and a constant sounding board throughout the writing of this book, Ashan was always willing to listen, challenge and reflect ideas back with clarity and care. Thanks mate. Those conversations mattered more than you know.

Scott Thomson, formerly Google's Innovation Lead in Australia, deserves a very special thank you. Scott is responsible for some of the most engaging conversations I have had about AI, the universe and everything. He also coined the deceptively simple idea that became 'the problem has the budget', a phrase that runs through this book because it captures something profoundly practical about how change really happens. Thank you for the thinking, the generosity and the timing.

I have been incredibly fortunate to work with outstanding clients while developing the ideas in this book. In particular, my work with **KPMG** in the United States and globally on AI strategy and transformation was instrumental in shaping much of the thinking here. I am grateful to leaders such as **Cliff Justice**, US Lead for Enterprise Innovation, **David Rowlands**, Global Head of AI, and **Stephen Chase**, Global Head of AI and Digital Innovation. You gave me the opportunity to explore what AI strategy and transformation look like at genuine global scale inside a driven, thoughtful and ambitious firm.

A special mention also goes to **Sarah Vega**, formerly Head of KPMG Futures, and **Charlie Wood** at Wiise, both of whom had the faith to work with Humanly Agile when we were still finding our feet. That early trust mattered more than you probably realised at the time.

Over the past two years, we have also been privileged to work with a number of exceptional organisations on AI strategy and transformation. Thank you to **Matt Aitken** and **Sean Smith** at **IVE Group**, **Anna Jackson** and **Kenan Hibberd** at **Unitywater**, and **Stephen Kowal** and **David Dekker** at **Atturra**. Each of you approached this work with seriousness, openness and a willingness to move beyond theory into practice. The lessons from that work are embedded throughout this book.

I also want to acknowledge **Jason Johnson** and **Jonathon Morse** from **Johnson Partners**, who were genuinely leading the way on AI agents while most organisations were still debating whether they were allowed to use them. You moved early, experimented responsibly and focused on building working systems rather than slideware. That leadership helped sharpen many of the ideas in this book and demonstrated what is possible when intent meets action.

A huge thank you to **Chelsea**, **Daniel**, **Jacky** and the entire team at **RelevanceAI**. You are a genuinely legendary Aussie startup and the builders of an AI agent platform we rely on daily – not theoretically, not occasionally, but in the real mess of client work and delivery. Your willingness to partner with us, move fast and treat practitioners as collaborators rather than customers has made it possible for us to bring agentic technology to our clients in a way that is practical, responsible and actually works.

Thank you as well to **Mike Smith**, **Jack Karikas** and **David Lewis** from **Mentorlist** for facilitating some of the most engaging, challenging and genuinely inspiring conversations with Australian CEOs I have had the pleasure of participating in. Those discussions, grounded in real leadership pressure rather than theory, were a constant reminder of what is actually at stake and helped keep this book anchored in reality.

Before closing, some final and very practical mentions. To my lawyer, **Peter Hodges**, who continues to save me from myself with remarkable consistency. Given the subject matter of this book, Peter is also one of the clearest real-world examples of expertise paired with empathy that I could hope to reference. He is calm, precise and unfailingly human when it matters most.

And to **Marcella** and **Rachada** and the team at Ink & Iris, thank you for once again producing a book cover design that is somehow both sharp and restrained, distinctive without shouting, and far better than the words inside deserve. You continue to make my work look smarter than it is.

Finally, my thanks to **Michael Hanrahan**, my publisher, and **Charlotte Duff**, my editor, who performed the minor miracle of turning my very average words into something printable. Your judgement, patience and ability to improve the work without sanding off its edges made this book materially better. I am deeply grateful to you both.

To everyone who challenged these ideas, tested them in the real world or simply asked better questions than I had answers for, thank you. This book exists because of those conversations, and any value in it belongs to the people who helped shape it.

www.ingramcontent.com/pod-product-compliance
Ingram Content Group Australia Pty Ltd
76 Discovery Rd, Dandenong South VIC 3175, AU
AUHW011020090426
425647AU00005B/5

9 781923 630208